Memory and Attention

Memory and Attention

An Introduction to Human Information Processing

DONALD A. NORMAN

University of California, San Diego

John Wiley & Sons, Inc.

NEW YORK · LONDON · SYDNEY · TORONTO

Preface

There are many reasons for writing books. This one could have been written to serve as a textbook, or as a source of reading selections for students, or as a vehicle for my own viewpoint about psychological processes. This book has been written for all of these reasons, and yet for none of them. The primary reason is that it has been fun to write.

The format of this book follows the format of a seminar, for that is how it has come into being. Basically, I have written what I have done (or wished I had done) during a seminar entitled "Memory and Attention." In a course, one hopes to give the student a feeling for the history of a subject, a working knowledge of the modern literature, and some grasp of the nature of the problems faced by the researchers in the field. This is accomplished by expository lectures, reading assignments, and critical evaluations of the literature. Throughout such a seminar, the temptation to add personal thoughts about the problems and their solutions is never resisted. I have tried to do the same things in this book.

This book is biased. It treats the human as a complex system, struggling to impose organization on the information received through the sense organs. This type of bias—always asking about the general structure of processes which the human uses to detect, recognize, attend to, and retain incoming information—allows me to organize in a meaningful way a good deal of our knowledge of the structure of human perception, attention, and memory. At the same time it makes it difficult, sometimes impossible, to discuss the more traditional psychological theories and experiments. As a result, the book consists of a very restricted survey of attention, memory, and pattern recognition. The restrictions are deliberate. I have tried to minimize the number of issues discussed in order that important ideas not be lost in a jumble of details.

Briefly, then, I introduce a broad selection of topics through a restricted set of papers and concepts. Most topics are discussed through excerpts from the original papers. Not only does it make little sense for me to paraphrase the words of the original, but much of the flavor of the field can only be experienced by reading the variety of styles and jargon used by the individual researchers. Some papers introduce the history of each area and its relation to other fields. The major effort, however, is concentrated on the examination of recent ideas and issues. Usually the modern work branches out in many directions and, of course, it is too early to tell which way the field will eventually develop. The works selected here are chosen to give the reader an understanding of each topic and some feeling for the problems and theories that can be used in its study. As a result, I have been somewhat arbitrary in my selection of studies, choosing them for their generality and the ease with which they could be inserted into the framework of the text.

Thus, the book does follow the seminar in many ways. Although one cannot provide a comprehensive survey of the literature in a single course, the hope is that the reader will end up with an understanding of the basic issues, an idea of where he can find more detailed information, and the ability to read the journals with understanding and insight. In keeping with the spirit of the seminar, I have reserved the right to comment and censor: eliminating from published writings whatever is irrelevant for the present context and making comments where appropriate.

This book is designed for the sophisticated beginner. No knowledge of psychology is assumed and technical terms are explained as they are introduced. Some of the problems are subtle, however, so that the complete novice to psychology may have difficulty. Many of the fields discussed here are now the subject of elaborate mathematical theories. I have resisted the temptation to elaborate on these models, primarily by promising to put them in a sequel, if ever there should be one.

I wish to thank George Mandler for his advice and encouragement during the construction of this book and, in general, simply for putting up with me. David Rumelhart has read all the chapters with care and his comments have helped to improve the final product. The format of this book, the frequent use of excerpts from the published literature, would not have been possible without the efforts of the authors from whose works I have selected. I wish to thank the publishers and authors of these papers for their permission to use these materials.

Donald A. Norman

La Jolla, California

Contents

Memory and Attention

1

The Problems

THE history of the formal study of human memory and attention is rich and varied. It is easy to trace a written record of speculation about these aspects of the human thought processes to the Greek philosophers, and the dedicated scholar could, no doubt, find earlier records. In fact, as early as 86–82 B.C. the Romans had a textbook of techniques for improving one's natural memory entitled *Rhetorica ad Herennium*. The rules given in *Ad Herennium* for establishing an "artificial" memory are still used today by practitioners of the art of memory, although since the invention of printing, this art is no longer of great value. To the Greeks and the Romans, rhetoric was an important part of life, and to the orator a reliable memory was of great importance. Today, with convenient access to libraries (and our acceptance of orators who speak from written notes), we have little need to memorize whole books, poems, or orations. Hence, the art of memory has fallen into disuse. But the rules established in the Greek and Roman world are still valid and useful today for those who wish to improve their memory. Modern science, with all its power, has added little to our knowledge about the practical art of remembering things.

The early practitioner of the art of memory realized that attention is a prerequisite of memory. In 400 B.C. the written rules of memory contained statements such as, "This is the first thing: if you pay attention, the judgment will better perceive the things going through it." [1] This simple quotation sets the stage for what follows. The orators wanted practical rules for improving their ability to use memory. Today, we

[1] My source for the early history of memory and for this quotation is the book *The Art of Memory*, by Frances A. Yates. Chicago: University of Chicago Press, 1966. Copyright 1966 by Frances A. Yates. We shall return to this topic in Chapter 6.

want understanding of the psychological principles which underlie the rules.

BASIC ISSUES

Let us start by reconsidering the quotation, "If you pay attention, the judgment will better perceive the things going through it." This is a common idea. We need to alter the words only slightly in order to recognize it in its modern form: "Now Jimmy, if you don't pay attention, you will never learn." The statement, we feel, must be true. What does it mean? What is this process called "attention"? What does it mean to start or stop paying attention? Obviously, the way we apply attention to one task or another is a psychological problem, for there is often no external sign that a person is or is not paying attention (although sometimes we stop paying attention by shutting our eyes or turning our heads).

What about perception? The quotation tells us that attention leads to better perception. Does this mean that if we place only half of our attention on a subject, we will perceive it only half as well? Now, immediately, we get to the heart of the whole problem. Can we consider attention to be a finely divisible process, sometimes putting 20 percent of its capacity to work on a problem and sometimes 70 percent? If so, what are we doing with the other 80 or 30 percent? Is attention something with a limited capacity which must be divided among the jobs at hand? Is perception a continuous process, dependent upon the amount of attention bestowed upon the objects to be perceived? The whole statement presupposes a particular mechanism of human processing.

This whole statement about the relationship of attention, perception and learning is quite unsatisfactory to the psychologist. Naming something "attention," something else "perception," and yet something else "learning," adds to our vocabulary, but not to our knowledge. The psychologist will not be satisfied until he can point to a specific process—that sequence of operations which performs transformations and makes decisions on sensory information—and identify this as a mechanism of attention. Then he tries to state the specific properties of each component of the overall process and show how they are related to other aspects of human abilities. The ultimate in specification is a model which describes in detail the operations which underlie attention, perception, learning, and memory.

In order to study the mechanics of human thought processes we must take a great leap in time from the Greek and Roman era to the 19th and 20th centuries. Although the phenomena have long been known, systematic scientific investigation of psychological processes has only recently begun. In the chapters that follow, we shall examine the progress of theories and experiments about the way humans process information by looking at two restricted fields: attention and memory. We do this by following the discussions of experimental psychologists, looking at some of their research, and discussing their theories. In so doing, it will be seen that even these two fields encompass a wide variety of problems, so many in fact that we divide them into many smaller subproblems. There is often little agreement about the proper breakdown of these problems, or even about the interpretation of the facts about any particular subproblem. It is often unclear how the theories proposed for each subproblem can ever be connected. These issues complicate the study of attention and memory, but they also enrich it. Modern psychology is a fascinating subject, not only because the subject matter is so interesting, but also because the area is so new and unexplored that all of us can take part in its development. So, although the apparent contradictions and gaps in the works that follow can be read with discouragement, they should be read with excitement. Ask yourself where the problems are and see if you can provide the extra bit of insight or evidence which would set them straight.

ORGANIZATION OF THE BOOK

Before we get into the subject matter, it may be useful to outline the overall organization of this book. The arrangement may be completely inaccurate as a model of human performance, but it is useful as a guide in understanding the problems that follow.

First, we view the human as a processor of information. In particular, we are concerned primarily with verbal, meaningful information in acoustical and visual form. The aim is to follow what happens to the information as it enters the human and is processed by the nervous system. The sense organs provide us with a picture of the physical world. Our problem is to interpret the sensory information and extract its psychological content. To do this we need to process the incoming signals and interpret them on the basis of our past experiences. Memory plays an active role in this process. It provides the information about the past necessary for proper understanding of the present. There must be temporary storage facilities to maintain the incoming information while it is being interpreted and it must be possible to add information about presently occurring events into permanent memory. We then make decisions and take actions on the information we have received.

Someplace along the line, the capacity of the human to deal with incoming information is severely limited. It is as if at some stage of the analysis of incoming information, only a small portion of the incoming signal is selected for further processing. The study of the phenomenon of attention is the study of this limitation and selection.

The procedure just described ignores the interconnections among the levels of processing. We would like to peel back the different levels one by one, starting with an understanding of the sensory organs, moving through sensation and perception and, finally, ending at decision making and thinking. Unfortunately, the trail ends soon after it starts. We have not yet finished the analysis of the most elementary level, sensation, and we have just barely started with perception. Beyond that, well, our lack of results is not from a lack of trying. One problem is that no process can be analyzed in isolation. We can, for example, analyze sensations only through the responses made by our experimental subjects, and these responses must be the result of the whole structure of their psychological processes, from sensation through decision making. It is only in recent years that we have learned to disentangle the sensory from the decision process. As a result of the fact that each level of psychological processing can be studied only through the other levels, our research in one field progresses slowly because it requires the simultaneous development of experimental skills and analytical techniques for understanding other fields.

The arrangement of this book follows the organization just described. We start with the problem of attention and the limits on our ability to process information (Chapter 2). Attention cannot be studied in isolation from other processes, so we proceed to a discussion of how sensory information can be identified and recognized as meaningful patterns (Chapter 3). The study of pattern recognition is still poorly developed, however, so we must be content with broad principles rather than specific facts. Both attention and pattern recognition depend heavily upon the properties of memory, so starting with Chapter 4 we study memory. It is convenient to examine the many different aspects of memory separately, although sometimes the divisions among the parts are arbitrary. We go from an examination of methodological difficulties to some proposals about the nature of a very limited sensory or very short-term memory (Chapter 4), to the study of short-term or primary memory (Chapter 5), to the examination of our large capacity, permanent memory system (Chapter 6).

After the structures of all these processes have been stated, we examine some of the general problems, asking how stored material is represented in memory and how storage is organized (Chapters 6 and 7). We discuss in some detail the practical art of remembering things— the mnemonics and memory systems of popular literature—for the study of tricks may yield some insight into the nature of memory itself. Finally, after some more general discussions, we conclude with an examination of formal models of memory and some speculations on the direction of future research and theories (Chapter 8).

One warning before we get down to business. The problem with studying mechanisms readily available to everyone's own inspection through introspection is that we cannot find out anything surprising. We spend years of careful research in the laboratory, meticulously separating the details of a process and experimentally determining the unreasonableness of alternative processes. When we finish, friends and students who are not psychologists say: "You mean it took you 10 years to discover that? I knew it all along, why didn't you ask me?" This can be rather discouraging. The answer to these comments is that there is a difference between the level of our understanding derived from careful experimentation and that derived from careless introspection. The one is precise and detailed, often mathematically specified and capable of accurate prediction and explanation. The other is vague and imprecise, lacking in detail and often conflicting with the opinions of others. That the two results do concern the same processes and usually confirm one another should be satisfying, not discomforting. It would be peculiar if our careful study of thought processes led to results which were at odds with all of our intuitions.

THE SUGGESTED READINGS

The readings and discussions contained in this book present a restricted survey of the literature and theoretical points of view in the fields of attention, memory, and pattern recognition. The restrictions are deliberate, both by personal biases and also to minimize the number of issues discussed in order that the important ideas not be lost in a jungle of details.

Although this policy is satisfactory for the purposes of introducing the problems of human information processing, it is not satisfactory for the student who has finished the book and wishes to continue his reading. Therefore, I have added a selected bibliography of references at the end of each chapter. These references are accompanied by a brief discussion of their importance. The bibliography is, of necessity, incomplete, but by emphasizing review articles, each reader will be able to rapidly focus upon the literature relevant to his particular interests. In addition, I have listed the specific journals which contain most of the new theoretical ideas for each particular field, so that the reader who wishes to see new developments will be able to skim the new literature quickly. Another procedure is to use the *Science Citation Index*, published quarterly by the Institute for Scientific Information, Inc., to find those newly published papers which reference the papers discussed in this book.

2

Attention

EVERY ONE knows what attention is. It is the taking possession by the mind, in clear and vivid form, of one out of what seems several simultaneously possible objects or trains of thought. Focalization, concentration, of consciousness are of its essence. It implies withdrawal from some things in order to deal effectively with others.[1]

We start with attention and with William James. William James was one of the first modern experimental psychologists (although he himself did few experiments). He believed in studying the mind by using every tool he could find: logic, introspection, and experimentation. His goal was to describe the functions of psychological processes, and he succeeded admirably. His massive textbook *The Principles of Psychology*, first published in 1890, makes good reading today.

As our first quotation from James states, the effects of attention are known by everyone. We cannot fully appreciate all that takes place at any one time. When we concentrate fully on a book, noises in the environment fade from consciousness; when our thoughts wander in a lecture, we find ourselves unable to recall the speaker's message, although we were aware that he was speaking. We can generate examples endlessly. Let us try rather to determine more exactly the nature of attention and the quantitative bounds on its limitations. Then, we may be able to construct the type of logical process that is involved in limiting and controlling attention.

[1] From William James, *The Principles of Psychology*, Vol. 1. New York: Henry Holt and Co., 1890. Pages 403–404.

THE PHENOMENA

William James deserves our study because he has carefully set forth his opinions about attention, letting us gain a deeper understanding of the many aspects of the phenomenon before we attempt to explain them. First, we follow James as he examines the problem of simultaneous attention. Granted that we have trouble attending to several simultaneous events, exactly how many items can we attend to at the same time? This problem is basic. We can immediately consider two different types of processes which might be responsible for the limitations of attention: one, a serial process which can do but one thing at a time, and the other, a parallel process which can do a number of things simultaneously, but with some upper limit to the total number of operations it can do at any one time.

A serial device requires some method of switching among the tasks that it is trying to do. If the switching can be performed with sufficient rapidity, there may be little loss in the information obtained from any given task. Parallel processes do not need to be switched from one task to another, but in turn, imply a good deal of complexity and redundancy in the mechanism that analyzes incoming information. The distinction between serial and parallel processes is of much current interest. Unfortunately, although James raises the issue, he gives us little help in resolving it, for he concludes that both possibilities might exist.[2]

ATTENTION *

WILLIAM JAMES

If, then, by the original question, how many ideas or things can we attend to at once, be meant how many entirely disconnected systems or processes

[2] In the readings that follow throughout the book, the original writings have been edited for continuity. Figures and footnotes have been renumbered to correspond to the numbers used here and occasional sentences referring to sections of the author's paper which are not included in this book have been deleted. The symbol − − − marks a deletion of material from a quotation. My comments are printed in the lighter style of type and lengthy quotations appear in the darker type.

* William James. The Principles of Psychology. Op. cit. Page 409.

of conception can go on simultaneously, the answer is, *not easily more than one, unless the processes are very habitual; but then two, or even three,* without very much oscillation of the attention. Where, however, the processes are less automatic, as in the story of Julius Caesar dictating four letters whilst he writes a fifth, there must be a rapid oscillation of the mind from one to the next, and no consequent gain of time. Within any one of the systems the parts may be numberless, but we attend to them collectively when we conceive the whole which they form.

The point seems to be that the number of things we can do depends upon the difficulty of each task. A well-learned task, such as walking, takes little effort and does not impede us in our performance of another. A more difficult task such as walking along a high, narrow ledge requires more concentration and may completely impede our efforts to hold a conversation.

Given that the number of things which we can attend to at once is very limited, what is our perception of events to which we are not attending? The act of switching our attention to an event may both blur our perception of that event and cause confusion in our judgments of its temporal properties. These are the critical observations for the experimental investigation of attention and they suggest a method of study. If attention is the result of a serial device, should there not be difficulty in determining the details and time sequence of events which occur during the absence of our attention? Again let us return to the descriptions of William James before we go to more modern versions.[3]

When the things to be attended to are small sensations, and when the effort is to be exact in noting them, it is found that attention to one interferes a good deal with the perception of the other. A good deal of fine work has been done in this field, of which I must give some account.

It has long been noticed, when expectant attention is concentrated upon one of two sensations, that the other one is apt to be displaced from consciousness for a moment and to appear subsequent; although in reality the two may have been contemporaneous events. Thus, to use the stock example of the books, the surgeon would sometimes see the blood flow from the arm of the patient whom he was bleeding, *before* he saw the instrument penetrate the skin. Similarly the smith may see the sparks fly *before* he sees the hammer smite the iron, etc. There is thus a certain difficulty in perceiving the exact *date* of two impressions when they do not interest our attention equally, and when they are of a disparate sort.

Professor Exner . . . makes some noteworthy remarks about the way in

[3] William James. *The Principles of Psychology, Op. cit.* Pages 409, 410, and 424–427.

which the attention must be *set* to catch the interval and the right order of the sensations, when the time is exceeding small. The point was to tell whether two signals were simultaneous or successive; and, if successive, which one of them came first.

The first way of attending which he found himself to fall into, was when the signals did not differ greatly—when, e.g., they were similar sounds heard each by a different ear. Here he lay in wait for the *first* signal, whichever it might be, and identified it the next moment in memory. The second, which could then always be known by default, was often not clearly distinguished in itself. When the time was too short, the first could not be isolated from the second at all.

The second way was to accommodate the attention for a certain *sort* of signal, and the next moment to become aware in memory of whether it came before or after its mate.

This way brings great uncertainty with it. The impression not prepared for comes to us in the memory more weak than the other, obscure as it were, badly fixed in time. We tend to take the subjectively stronger stimulus, that which we were intent upon, for the first, just as we are apt to take an objectively stronger stimulus to be the first. Still, it may happen otherwise. In the experiments from touch to sight it often seemed to me if the impression for which the attention was *not* prepared were there already when the other came.

Exner found himself employing this method oftenest when the impressions differed strongly.

— — —

THE EFFECTS OF ATTENTION

Its remote effects are too incalculable to be recorded. The practical and theoretical life of whole species, as well as of individual beings, results from the selection which the habitual direction of their attention involves.

— — —

Suffice it meanwhile that each of us literally *chooses*, by his ways of attending to things, what sort of a universe he shall appear to himself to inhabit.

The immediate effects of attention are to make us:

(a) perceive
(b) conceive
(c) distinguish
(d) remember

better than otherwise we could—both more successive things and each thing more clearly. It also

t a sensation attended to becomes
point is, however, not quite plain,
ɔm the strength or intensity of a
ɪs; and to increase *this* is, for some
ɪ do. When the facts are surveyed,
extent the relative intensity of two
them is attended to and the other
e a scene before his eyes appear
he way he sets his attention. If for
start out of everything; if for cold,
notes in a chord, or overtones in a
ɔunds probably a little more loud
ɪefore. When we mentally break a
m, by accentuating every second or
stress of attention is laid seems to
ic. The increased visibility of optical
ːh close attention brings about, can
a real strengthening of the retinal
ːndered particularly probable by the
ː, if attention be concentrated upon
ɪ eye almost the brilliancy of reality,
y gifted observers) leave a negative
y. Confident expectation of a certain
ɪnːeɪɪsɪɪy ɔɪ quulɪɪy ɔɪ ɪmɪɔɪɪɪɪ   ten make us sensibly see or hear it
in an object which really falls far short of it. In face of such facts it is rash
to say that attention cannot make a sense-impression more intense.

But, on the other hand, the intensification which may be brought about
seems never to lead the judgment astray. As we rightly perceive and name
the same color under various lights, the same sound at various distances; so
we seem to make an analogous sort of allowance for the varying amounts
of attention with which objects are viewed; and whatever changes of feeling
the attention may bring we charge, as it were, to the attention's account, and
still perceive and conceive the object as the same.

A gray paper appears to us no lighter, the pendulum-beat of a clock no louder,
no matter how much we increase the strain of our attention upon them. No one, by
doing this, can make the gray paper look white, or the stroke of the pendulum sound
like the blow of a strong hammer—everyone, on the contrary, feels the increase as that
of his own conscious activity turned upon the thing.

Were it otherwise, we should not be able to note *intensities* by attending
to them. Weak impressions would, as Stumpf says, become stronger by the
very fact of being observed.

I should not be able to observe faint sounds at all, but only such as appeared to me of maximal strength, or at least of a strength that increased with the amount of my observation. In reality, however, I can, with steadily increasing attention, follow a diminuendo perfectly well.

The subject is one which would well repay exact experiment, if methods could be devised. Meanwhile there is no question whatever that attention augments the *clearness* of all that we perceive or conceive by its aid. But what is meant by clearness here?

c.   *Clearness,* so far as attention produces it, *means distinction from other things* and *internal analysis or subdivision.* These are essentially products of intellectual *discrimination,* involving comparison, memory, and perception of various relations. The attention *per se* does not distinguish and analyze and relate. The most we can say is that it is a condition of our doing so. And as these processes are to be described later, the clearness they produce had better not be farther discussed here. The important point to notice here is that it is not attention's *immediate* fruit.

d.   Whatever future conclusion we may reach as to this, we cannot deny that *an object once attended to will remain in the memory,* whilst one inattentively allowed to pass will leave no traces behind.

William James leaves us with a very complete description of the phenomenon of attention. He describes its variety, its nature, and its effects. Not much can be added to the overall picture, but all of the details must be filled in. We have just read that attention can alter the temporal order of our perceptions; why? We have read that attention affects retention, clarity, and reaction time; why? Even with a good description of the phenomenon we still know little of the mechanism.

Attention received much study following William James. Eighteen years later, in 1908, Edward B. Titchener wrote from his experimental laboratory at Cornell that one of the few things psychology could credit itself with achieving was the discovery of attention. Titchener credited the German introspectionist Wundt with the doctrine of attention, dating its inception as 1860, but, commenting further on the critical importance of attention, Titchener pointed out that "the discovery of attention did not result in any immediate triumph of the experimental method. It was something like the discovery of a hornet's nest: the first touch brought out a whole swarm of insistent problems." (Titchener, 1908, Chapter 5.)

Titchener tried hard to specify the attributes of attention by such "laws" as the law of prior entry in which he stated that, "the stimulus for which we are predisposed requires less time than a like stimulus, for which we are unprepared, to produce its full conscious effect. Or, in popular terms, the object of attention comes to consciousness more quickly than the objects that we are not attending to." But Titchener was forced to conclude that, "although the discovery of a reliable measure of attention would appear to be one of the most important problems that await solution by the experimental psychology of the future" (Titchener quoting Külpe), "the discovery has not yet been made." All these statements apply today, some sixty years later.

The study of attention declined from the early years of the century until the 1950's. Then, in England, a group of researchers started a whole new series of studies, this time with a specific theoretical model of the attention process in mind. Several dramatic changes in scientific technique had occurred in those interim years. Mostly as a result of tremendous impetus to scientific work produced by the second world war, communication engineers had developed powerful electronic systems and analytical techniques, including the digital computer and related topics in automata and network theory.

SELECTIVE ATTENTION AND THE COCKTAIL PARTY PROBLEM

One of the first studies to come out of the new era of experimentation exemplifies many of the characteristics of the research. It was conducted by an Englishman, E. Colin Cherry, in an American laboratory at the Massachusetts Institute of Technology. The study was one of experimental psychology, but it was performed in the MIT Research Laboratory of Electronics and was published in a physics journal, the *Journal of the Acoustical Society of America*. Such interdisciplinary research is characteristic of modern psychology.

Cherry addressed himself to the problem of selective attention, or as he put it, "the cocktail party problem." The cocktail party serves as a fine example of selective attention. We stand in a crowded room with sounds and conversations all about us. Often the conversation to which we are trying to listen is not the one in which we are supposedly taking part. There are many different aspects of the cocktail party to interest psychologists. (We ignore the idea that it is a comfortable way in which to conduct research.) First, what is our selective ability? How are we able to select the one voice that interests us out of the many that surround us? Second, how much do we retain of the conversations to which we do not pay attention?

The first problem, selective attention, is not trivial. It implies a very complex analysis of the sounds which arrive at our ears—an analysis so complex that it cannot yet be performed by electronic devices. The second problem, the measure of our knowledge of rejected sources of speech, tells us how well the attention mechanism selects and rejects channels of information. These two problems, we will see, characterize the most recent research, for they are at the core of the phenomenon: we select what is relevant; we reject the rest.

As you read Cherry's paper, note several things. First, humans use all the information that is available in performing their tasks. When we are required to separate two simultaneously spoken messages we do so by physical cues such as the idiosyncrasies of the speakers' voices, their spatial location, their intensities, and whatever else we can find to distinguish them. If these physical cues fail, we use psychological ones, such as the grammatical or semantic content of the spoken material. If we are asked to specify just what aspect of the situation allows a human to select one voice from others, we cannot give a simple answer. Second, note that Cherry's experiments indicate that his subjects knew little of the characteristics of the rejected channel, but as you read his convincing demonstration of this fact, ask yourself how we are able to switch our attention to new voices or events when the occasion arises, if we are unaware of the content of those other events. The inconsistency between our apparent lack of knowledge of rejected channels and our selective ability, governs the conclusions and studies of the rest of this chapter.

SOME EXPERIMENTS ON THE RECOGNITION OF SPEECH, WITH ONE AND WITH TWO EARS *

E. COLIN CHERRY

INTRODUCTION

The tests to be described are in two groups. In the first, two different spoken messages are presented to the subject simultaneously, using both ears. In the

* E. Colin Cherry. Some experiments on the recognition of speech, with one and with two ears. *Journal of the Acoustical Society of America,* 1953, 25, 975–979. Copyright 1953 by the Acoustical Society of America. With permission of author and publisher.

second, one spoken message is fed to his right ear and a different message to his left ear. The results, the subject's spoken reconstructions, are markedly different in the two cases; so also are the significances of these results. Before examining such possible significance, it will be better to describe some of the experiments.

THE SEPARATION OF TWO SIMULTANEOUSLY SPOKEN MESSAGES

The first set of experiments relates to this general problem of speech recognition: how do we recognize what one person is saying when others are speaking at the same time (the "cocktail party problem")? On what logical basis could one design a machine ("filter") for carrying out such an operation? A few of the factors which give mental facility might be the following:

(a) The voices come from different directions.
(b) Lip-reading, gestures, and the like.
(c) Different speaking voices, mean pitches, mean speeds, male and female, and so forth.
(d) Accents differing.
(e) Transition-probabilities (subject matter, voice dynamics, syntax . . .).

All of these factors, except the last (e), may, however, be eliminated by the device of recording two messages on the same magnetic-tape, spoken by the same speaker. The result is a babel, but nevertheless the messages may be separated.

— — —

At the subjective level the subject reported very great difficulty in accomplishing his task. He would shut his eyes to assist concentration. Some phrases were repeatedly played over by him, perhaps 10 to 20 times, but his guess was right in the end. In no cases were any long phrases (more than 2 or 3 words) identified wrongly.

In a variation of the experiment the subject was given a pencil and paper, and permitted to write down the words and phrases as he identified them. Subjectively speaking, his task then became "very much easier." Times were shortened. It appears that the long-term storage provided assists prediction.

Numerous tests have been made, using pairs of messages of varying similarity. Some test samples consisted of adjacent paragraphs out of the same book. The results were consistently similar; the messages were almost entirely separated.

However, it was considered possible to construct messages which could not be separated with such a low frequency of errors. Such a test is described in the next Section.

INSEPARABLE SPOKEN MESSAGES. USE OF CLICHÉS OR "HIGHLY-PROBABLE PHRASES"

As a final test in this series, using the same speaker recorded as speaking two different messages simultaneously, a pair of messages was composed which could not be separated by the listening subject. The messages were composed by selecting, from reported speeches in a newspaper, 150 clichés and stringing them together with simple conjunctions, pronouns, etc., as continuous speeches. For example, a few of the clichés were:

(1) I am happy to be here today,
(2) The man in the street,
(3) Stop beating about the bush,
(4) We are on the brink of ruin,

and the like. The corresponding sample of one speech was as follows:

"I am happy to be here today to talk to the man in the street. Gentlemen, the time has come to stop beating about the bush—we are on the brink of ruin, and the welfare of the workers and of the great majority of the people is imperiled," and so forth.

It is remarkably easy to write such passages by the page. Now a cliché is, almost by definition, a highly probable chain of words, and on the other hand the transition probability of one cliché following another specific one is far lower. The subject, as he listened to the mixed speeches in an endeavor to separate one of them was observed to read out complete clichés at a time; it appeared that recognition of one or two words would insure his predicting a whole cliché. But he picked them out in roughly equal numbers from both speeches; in such artificially constructed cases, message separation appeared impossible. The speeches were of course read with normal continuity, and with natural articulatory and emotional properties, during their recording.

It is suggested that techniques such as those described in the preceding sections may be extended so that they will shed light on the relative importance of the different types of transition probabilities in recognition. For instance, speeches of correct "syntactical structure" but with no meaning and using few dictionary words may readily be constructed. [Lewis Carroll's "Jabberwocky" is such an instance; similarly, "meaningful" speeches with almost zero (or at least unfamiliar) syntactical or inflexional structure (Pidgin English).] Again continuous speaking of dictionary words, which are relatively disconnected, into "meaningless phrases" is possible; the word-transition probabilities may be assessed a priori, with the assistance of suitable probability tables. Further experiments are proceeding.[4]

[4] Some of Cherry's further experiments are reported in Cherry and Taylor, 1954.

UNMIXED SPEECHES; ONE IN THE LEFT EAR AND ONE IN THE RIGHT

The objective, and subjective, results of a second series of tests were completely different. In these tests one continuous spoken message was fed into a headphone on the subject's left ear and a different message applied to the right ear. The messages were recorded, using the same speaker.

The subject experiences no difficulty in listening to either speech at will and "rejecting" the unwanted one. Note that aural directivity does not arise here; the earphones are fixed to the head in the normal way. To use a loose expression, the "processes of recognition may apparently be switched to either ear at will." This result has surprised a number of listeners; although of course it is well known to anyone who has made hearing tests. It may be noteworthy that when one tries to follow the conversation of a speaker in a crowded noisy room, the instinctive action is to turn one ear toward him, although this may increase the difference between the "messages" reaching the two ears.

The subject is instructed to repeat one of the messages concurrently while he is listening (Broadbent, 1952) and to make no errors. Surprising as it may seem this proves easy; his words are slightly delayed behind those on the record to which he is listening. One marked characteristic of his speaking voice is its monotony. Very little emotional content or stressing of the words occurs at all. Subjectively, the subject is unaware of this fact. Also he may have very little idea of what the message that he has repeated is all about, especially if the subject matter is difficult. But he has recognized every word, as his repeating proves.

But the point of real interest is that if the subject is subsequently asked to repeat anything of what he heard in his other (rejected-message) ear, he can say little about it at all, except possibly that sounds were occurring.

Experiments were made in an attempt to find out just what attributes, if any, of the "rejected" message are recognized.

LANGUAGE OF "REJECTED" EAR UNRECOGNIZED

In a further set of tests the two messages, one for the right ear and one for the left, started in English. After the subject was comfortably repeating his right-ear message, the left-ear message was changed to German, spoken by an Englishman. The subject subsequently reported, when asked to state the language of the "rejected" left-ear message, that he "did not know at all, but assumed it was English." The test was repeated with different, unprepared listeners; the results were similar. It is considered unfair to try this particular test more than once with the same listener.

It was considered that a further series of tests might well indicate the level of recognition which is attained in the "rejected" ear, raising the questions, Is the listener aware even that it is human speech? male or female? and the like.

WHAT FACTORS OF THE "REJECTED" MESSAGE ARE RECOGNIZED

In this series of tests the listening subjects were presented at their right-hand ears with spoken passages from newspapers, chosen carefully to avoid proper names or difficult words, and again instructed to repeat these passages concurrently without omission or error. Into their left ears were fed signals of different kinds, for different tests, but each of which started and ended with a short passage of normal English speech in order to avoid any troubles that might be involved in the listener's "getting going" on the test. The center, major, portions of these rejected left-ear signals thus reached the listener while he was steadily repeating his right-ear message.

Again no one listening subject was used for more than one test; none of them was primed as to the results to be expected. The center, major, portions of the left-ear signals for the series of tests were, respectively:

(a) Normal male spoken English—as for earlier tests.

(b) Female spoken English—high-pitched voice.

(c) Reversed male speech (i.e., same spectrum but no words or semantic content).

(d) A steady 400-cps oscillator.

After any one of these tests, the subject was asked the following questions:

(1) Did the left-ear signal consist of human speech or not?

(2) If yes is given in answer to (1), can you say what it was about, or even quote any words?

(3) Was it a male or female speaker?

(4) What language was it in?

The responses varied only slightly. In no case in which normal human speech was used did the listening subjects fail to identify it as speech; in every such instance they were unable to identify any word or phrase heard in the rejected ear and, furthermore, unable to make definite identification of the language as being English. On the other hand the change of voice—male to female—was nearly always identified while the 400-cps pure tone was always observed. The reversed speech was identified as having "something queer about it" by a few listeners, but was thought to be normal speech by others.

The broad conclusions are that the "rejected" signal has certain statistical properties recognized, but that detailed aspects, such as the language, individual words, or semantic content are unnoticed.

EXPERIMENTS AND EARLY THEORIES

Cherry's research has introduced a new phenomenon and a new experimental technique. Let us review this technique briefly, for it will play an increasingly important role in later sections of this chapter. The technique is to require a subject to repeat a message which is presented to him—to *shadow* the message—while at the same time he is presented with other material, either auditorally or visually. Cherry reports that the task of shadowing is easy, but also that "one marked characteristic of (the subject's) speaking voice is its monotony. Very little emotional content or stressing of the words occurs at all . . . he may have very little idea of what the message that he has repeated is all about." Cherry's description of the subject's tone of voice and inability to remember what had been shadowed suggests a difficult task. Actually, the task of shadowing can be made either easy or difficult, depending upon the details of the way it is performed.

The critical variables involved in shadowing are of two forms: the instructions given to the subject and the type of material that is being shadowed. The type of material is important, for if a passage of prose is selected from a novel, the task is easier than if the material is from a technical work. Both these selections are grammatical; the shadowing task becomes even more difficult if the material consists of randomly arranged English words, and harder yet, with nonsense words. The importance of the grammatical aspects of the material cannot be over-emphasized. The first part of Cherry's paper shows that even in the absence of physical cues, two different speeches mixed together can be disentangled if there are sufficient grammatical constraints involved. When the grammatical constraints are relaxed by using speeches constructed of clichés or nonmeaningful phrases, separation of the messages becomes very difficult or impossible. Even when the speeches to be separated are accompanied by physical cues, such as being presented to different ears or being read in separate voices, grammatical structure plays an important role in the ability to attend to one while rejecting the other. We would not survive at the cocktail party were the speech of the participants completely devoid of grammatical structure or meaning. We shall return to this issue later, for the structure imposed on verbal messages by the rules of grammar and meaning play an important role in recent theories of attention.

Cherry reports that his subject's "words are slightly delayed behind those on the record to which he is listening." We call this type of behavior *phrase shadowing*, and it simplifies the task for the subject. Indeed, skilled typists, readers, or Morse Code receivers learn to type, speak, or write with a considerable lag between what they produce and what they receive or see. The longer the lag, the greater the advantage that can be taken of the structure of language, and the easier the task becomes, whether it be the laboratory exercise of shadowing or the similar practical job of typing or reading aloud. We can tremendously increase the difficulty involved in shadowing by instructing subjects to stop phrase shadowing and start *phonemic shadowing*. In phonemic shadowing, the subject is required to repeat each sound as he hears it, without waiting for the completion of a phrase, or indeed, without waiting for the completion of a word. Phonemic shadowing is difficult to do; it takes a lot of practice for subjects to learn how and even then they usually cannot do it without error.

Shadowing, then, is a powerful but complicated experimental task. It has many problems as a laboratory tool in the study of attention because it is difficult to measure just how much effort the subject uses in performing the shadowing. The list of variables which influence shadowing illustrate that a simple tabulation of how accurately the subject's spoken words agree with the presented material does not even begin to tell us how much attention is diverted to the task. Cherry suggests some of the other measures we might have to use. Is not the inability of subjects to remember the content of the shadowed message a statement of its difficulty? Here the act of shadowing must have interfered only with memory, not perception, because the fact that the shadowing was accurate proves that every word of the passage was perceived properly. Why, then, is there little memory for it? The fact that Cherry's subjects used phrase shadowing indicates that memory was involved; some memory had to store each word between the time it arrived at the ears and the time it was spoken by the subject. Phrase shadowing implies that there is a grammatical analysis of the material being processed. With all this memory and analysis, we must conclude, surprisingly enough, that although Cherry places maximum emphasis on the "rejection" of information from the nonshadowed channel, material which was shadowed is also "rejected," at least to some extent.

When Cherry tested subjects on their ability to recognize the language of the material presented on the "rejected" channel, he stated that "it is considered unfair to try this particular test more than once with the same listener." Unfair? If shadowing truly diverts the attention from the material presented on the other channel, why should it be unfair to use a listener in the same test several times? Is it unfair because after a while the listener would be able to say what language had been presented? If so, just what is taking place when a subject shadows; can he selectively accept or reject other material?

This discussion should not be read as a criticism of Cherry's experiments. The discussion is only intended to emphasize some of the difficulties involved in doing research on attention and to spell out some new theoretical issues. The effects Cherry reports are dramatic ones. In a later series of experiments, the psychologist Moray (1959) has tried to determine exactly how much information humans retain of the rejected channel. He found that even when English words were repeated as many as 35 times in the rejected ear, there was absolutely no retention of them. Even when the subjects were told that they were later to be tested on their retention of material from the nonshadowed ear it made little difference; the task of shadowing was so difficult that it completely distracted their attention from other material.

There are several possible explanations of these results. The inability of subjects to recall much information about material on the non-shadowed channel might be the result of masking: the sounds of the message which is to be shadowed combined with the subject's voice as he repeats that message drown out or mask the voice which speaks the other message. There are several reasons, however, why this is probably not correct. The simplest reasons (though by no means all that might be given) come from the introspections of subjects and from a simple logical analysis of the experiment.

The logical analysis proceeds as follows: we can present the speech from both information channels over one loudspeaker. When we do this, the word which is about to be shadowed is interfered with by both the word coming from the other, nonshadowed speech and the word which the subject is in the process of speaking. The word in the nonshadowed message is, similarly, interfered with by both the voice of the subject and the word being spoken on the message which is to be shadowed. Thus, the total amount of interference is the same for both channels, yet one channel is perceived—the subject shadows it properly, and the other channel is not—the subject recalls very little about its properties.[5]

[5] This argument neglects the effect of grammatical context on the ease with which a message can be perceived, even with interference. It is easier to understand material which fits within a grammatical context than ungrammatical material. The

The easiest way to dispel any possible alternative explanation for the result is to try the task. The impression one receives is quite clearly that of a limited ability to process the material. It is as if you attend to the total speech input only in order to latch on to the desired speech. Then, you dare not release your attention from the message you are shadowing even for an instant, for if you do, you will not be able to maintain perfect shadowing. Even though the sounds and words from the nonshadowed message are heard, they pass by without leaving any lasting impression.

There is still one other difficulty with the observation that little or nothing is remembered of the nonshadowed task. Both Cherry and Moray waited a while before asking their subjects how much they remembered of the nonattended material. James hints at the problem when he tells us that "an object once attended to will remain in the memory, whilst one inattentively allowed to pass will leave no traces behind." Does that mean that even the object which receives no attention is remembered briefly before its traces disappear? To answer this question is simple; we need only interrupt the subject while he is shadowing and quickly demand of him what was presented on the ear which he was not shadowing. This is what we might call the "what-did-you-say" phenomenon. Often when someone to whom you were not "listening" asks a question of you, your first reaction is to say, "uh, what did you say?" But then, before the question is repeated, you can dredge it up yourself from memory. When this experiment was actually tried in my laboratory (Norman, 1969), the results agreed with our intuitions: there is a temporary memory for items to which we are not attending, but, as Cherry, James, and Moray point out, no long-term memory.

The first complete theory of attention came in 1958 by Donald Broadbent, from the psychological laboratories in Cambridge, England. Broadbent developed a series of experiments, the most famous involving simultaneous memorization of two simultaneously presented sequences of digits.[6]

shadowed message presumably is a grammatical message, whereas, the nonshadowed message, in the absence of effort to understand it, is essentially a list of isolated words, poorly remembered. Nonetheless, the masking argument is not very convincing.

[6] A glossary of terminology might be appropriate here. In experiments involving auditory information presented to the two ears, it is necessary to distinguish among the various ways in which that information might be presented.

Consider two sources of sounds, A and B, which we wish to present simultaneously to a listener. If A and B are both presented to one ear only (through an earphone) we say that the presentation is *monaural*. If A and B are mixed together

When Broadbent presented his subjects with three pairs of digits dichotically, so that one set of three digits read serially was heard at one ear at the same time as a second set of digits was heard at the other ear, he found surprising results. First, his subjects could barely recall 4 or 5 digits, whereas in more normal situations people have little trouble in remembering a string of 7 to 10 digits. Second, subjects preferred to organize their output by ears, rather than by the apparently more natural order, the order in which they heard the digits. That is, if the right ear has presented to it the digits 1, 7, 6, at the rate of one digit every half-second and the left ear the digits 8, 5, 2, the actual order of presentation of the digits is by the three pairs 1–8; 7–5; and 6–2. The preferred order of recall, however, is to give one ear's sequence first and then the other's: 1, 7, 6 and then 8, 5, 2. Usually, subjects get all the digits correct from the first ear, but make errors in the other sequence.

What can we make of these results? Broadbent concluded that they illustrated the properties of selective attention; selection was made on the basis of the physical channels by which the digits were presented. After considering a large set of experimental findings of various sorts, including the dichotically presented digits and Cherry's results, Broadbent put together a theoretical structure which he felt represented the underlying processes.

THE FILTER MODEL

Broadbent was attempting to piece together a model of human capability that would account for a wide variety of data, not just those from experiments in attention. Basically, Broadbent suggested that the limit to our ability to perceive competing messages is perceptual; we are able to analyze and identify only a limited amount of the information which arrives at our sensory inputs. He proposed that the brain contains a "selective filter" which can be "tuned" to accept the desired message and "reject" all others. The filter thus manages to block undesired inputs,

and then presented to both ears, so that both ears hear exactly the same material, we say the presentation is *binaural*. If the two channels are fed into separate ears, so that the left ear hears only A and the right ear only B, we say the presentation is *dichotic*. Finally, if we feed A through one loudspeaker and B through another placed nearby in such a way as to recreate the sound patterns resulting when two persons might simultaneously take the part of A and B, we say the presentation is *stereophonic*. Similar distinctions can be made for visual material: *monoptic, dioptic, stereoscopic*.

reducing the processing load on the perceptual system. In the following excerpt from this book, Broadbent summarizes the model and tries to show how it is compatible with the evidence from a rather wide variety of psychological tasks. His model is important, for it shaped the direction for further research in attention. It is appropriate that we review it now, before we examine other, later experiments.

PERCEPTION AND COMMUNICATION *

DONALD E. BROADBENT

SUMMARY OF PRINCIPLES

(a) A nervous system acts to some extent as a single communication channel, so that it is meaningful to regard it as having a limited capacity.

(b) A selective operation is performed upon the input to this channel, the operation taking the form of selecting information from all sensory events having some feature in common. Physical features identified as able to act as a basis for this selection include the intensity, pitch, and spatial localization of sounds.

(c) The selection is not completely random, and the probability of a particular class of events being selected is increased by certain properties of the events and by certain states of the organism.

(d) Properties of the events which increase the probability of the information, conveyed by them, passing the limited capacity channel include the following: physical intensity, time since the last information from that class of events entered the limited capacity channel, high frequency of sounds as opposed to low (in man).

— — —

(h) Incoming information may be held in a temporary store at a stage previous to the limited capacity channel: it will then pass through the channel when the class of events to which it belongs is next selected. The maximum time of storage possible in this way is of the order of seconds.

(i) To evade the limitations of (h) it is possible for information to return to temporary store after passage through the limited capacity channel: this

* Donald E. Broadbent. Perception and Communication. London: Pergamon Press, 1958. Pages 297–300. Copyright 1958 by D. E. Broadbent. With permission of author and publisher.

provides storage of unlimited time at the cost of reducing the capacity of the channel still further and possibly to zero. (Long-term storage does not affect the capacity of the channel, but rather is the means for adjusting the internal coding to the probabilities of external events; so that the limit on the channel is an informational one and not simply one of a number of simultaneous stimuli.)

(j) A shift of the selective process from one class of events to another takes a time which is not negligible compared with the minimum time spent on any one class.

— — —

An information-flow diagram incorporating the more probable principles is shown in Fig. 1.

— — —

Major Implications of These Principles

Now that these principles are stated thus baldly, it may be urged that they are not particularly surprising. Do we not know that attention is limited, that noises distract us, that we consciously rehearse any matter which must be remembered for a short period, and so on? What gain is there from putting these everyday experiences into this stilted language? They have already been formulated by the classical introspective psychologists: why is time and effort wasted on rephrasing them?

There are two answers to this objection. First, it is indeed true that the principles lead to no prediction which is contrary to everyday observation.

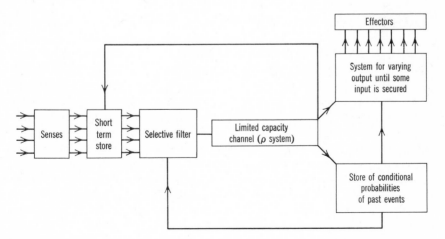

Fig. 1. A tentative information-flow diagram for the organism, as conceived at the present time.

It would be a poor set of scientific principles which did do so: though it is not uncommon for psychologists to feel that they ought to contradict common beliefs about behaviour.

But secondly, as a matter of history it is not true that these principles are obvious nor that they were adequately formulated by classical psychologists. It is quite possible to say that mentalistic statements are consistent with them: to say that our limited capacity single channel is to be equated with the unitary attention of the introspectionists. Indeed, the writer believes that the one is simply a more exact version of the other. But a view of attention as unitary might also be taken to mean that a man cannot perform two tasks at once: which experimental evidence shows to be untrue. A view of noise as distracting might be taken to mean that card-sorting or mental arithmetic will be worse performed in noise, which they are not.

Broadbent provides us with a complete structure for selection and attention which agrees with intuition and with the facts known at that time (1958). Basically the hypothesis can be summarized by saying that a limited capacity processor deals with but one channel of information at a time. The human selects among the various sources of information impinging on his sense organs on the basis of the physical characteristics of the information. When necessary, he switches attention among the various input sources. A short-term memory system prevents loss of information about the immediate past history of the unselected channels.

THE FILTER MODEL FAILS AND IS MODIFIED

Broadbent's theory indicated a specific theoretical structure which, in turn, had strong implications on how people behave. Some of these implications were tested and proved wrong. One method of probing the theoretical structure is by means of the question raised earlier with Cherry's paper: how are we able to switch our attention among inputs if we are unaware of the content of unselected inputs?

A crucial experiment on this point was done by two undergraduates at Oxford, Gray and Wedderburn (1960). They rejected the idea that attention was based on the physical characteristics of sensory channels and suggested that psychological attributes played an important role in selection. Their experiments were simple in concept but the results were devastating to Broadbent's theory. Suppose we listened to one word so divided that different syllables of the word are presented alternately to different ears. At the same time, another word is decomposed in a similar fashion and presented to the complementary ear. Would not the attention switch from ear to ear and, thus, recreate each word correctly, rather than stick to one physical channel and get a nonsensical mixture of syllables? If this is so—and Gray and Wedderburn showed that it is—the attention mechanism must be able to extract the meaning of information from the two ears in order to know which to choose. But Broadbent's system (Fig. 1) requires attention to be switched at an early stage in the processing of sensory information, much before any of the meaning has been extracted.

The distinction between selection on the basis of physical or sensory analyses and selection on the basis of a more thorough analysis of meaning is very important. Broadbent's theoretical scheme makes good sense; we would not like to discard the overall structure. Yet it is clear from even the simple points raised by Gray and Wedderburn that something is wrong. A much more complete discussion of this problem was put forth by Anne Treisman in her doctoral dissertation at Oxford University in 1961. Treisman examined the role of verbal and linguistic features on her subjects' ability to select one message from among several. In particular, she hoped to test Broadbent's suggestion that "classes" of words may behave in the same way as sensory channels do by presenting messages in different languages. Certainly a difference in language is an extreme case of a verbal distinction between two messages without any general differences in physical characteristics. In addition, she examined the role of familiarity, redundancy, meaningfulness, and similarity.

Treisman evaluated Broadbent's theory of a selective filter by continuing and elaborating on Cherry's experimental methods. The technique of this research is to keep the subject occupied performing a shadowing task while various types of competing messages and signals are presented to him. It has been found that, if the subject manages to keep up the shadowing task, gross physical changes of the nonshadowed message are noticed (change from a man's voice to a woman's), simple changes are not noticed (changes in the language of the nonshadowed message), and "important" words on the nonshadowed ear are often noticed (the subject's name or material which would be relevant within the context of the shadowed material).

The problem discussed for the rest of the chapter deals with the way in which our ability to perceive material is limited. The selective filter proposed by Broadbent works to minimize the amount of processing that must be performed by more complex, higher level processes. Broadbent evidently had in mind an ascending chain of complexity with some central mechanism performing the final analysis on incoming information. In this scheme one wants to eliminate irrelevant messages from the central mechanism. The problem, as we shall see, is that the properties required of the filter became so complex that the filter seemed to be almost as complicated as the final mechanism it was attempting to serve.

In her experiments, Treisman studied selective attention to one of two competing messages, presented binaurally. The messages were created by varying a number of different attributes. The irrelevant material was sometimes read with the same voice as the relevant material (female) and sometimes in a different voice (male). The nature of the irrelevant material also varied, sometimes being a technical discussion, other times passages from novels, and sometimes passages from the same novel as the relevant channel. Finally, the language of the irrelevant passage varied from English to Latin, French, German, and Czech (with a deliberate English accent), to English played backward over the tape recorder, and even to a French translation of the English shadowed message. The subjects' job was to shadow the relevant channel and ignore entirely the irrelevant material. As we can guess from Cherry's study, this is an easy task when the voices and materials used for the two messages are different, but a difficult task when the same voices and similar materials are used.

The aim of these studies, remember, was to determine at what level the selection of relevant from irrelevant material was made. Broadbent postulated selection almost entirely based on sensory features. Treisman hoped that by using a variety of irrelevant material she could distinguish between the relative effects of cues based entirely on sensory features and cues which required the determination of familiarity and meaning. Her experiments showed that sensory cues alone were not sufficient. She summarized her results and put forth a hypothesis to account for the types of errors made by her subjects (Ss) in this way:

VERBAL CUES IN SELECTIVE ATTENTION *

ANNE M. TREISMAN

(1) It was shown that a difference in voice (male vs. female) and a difference in language have quite different effects on tasks requiring selective response

* Anne M. Treisman. Verbal cues, language and meaning in selective attention. Amer. J. Psychol., 1964, 77, 215–216. Copyright 1965 by Karl H. Dallenbach. With permission of author and publisher.

to one of two messages. The difference in voice allows the irrelevant message to be rejected much more efficiently, and this probably takes place at an earlier stage in the perceptual analysis of inputs. (2) When two messages share the same general physical characteristics, a difference in language allows some selection between them; however this seems more similar to selection between two English messages on the basis of subject matter than to the efficient performance obtained with different voices. Thus, complete rejection of one language as such appears to be impossible. (3) Phonetic cues make an unknown foreign language less distracting than a message which is phonetically similar to English (the Czech nonsense), and allow the Ss to name the irrelevant foreign language. Reversed speech however, causes a relatively high degree of interference. (4) The Ss' knowledge of the language affects the amount of interference it produces. In most cases, however, little of the content of the rejected message can be reported. Many Ss failed to notice that the Czech was not normal English and not all the Ss, even among those who knew the language fluently, realize that a rejected French message was a translation of the selected English one. While similarity of the languages at the phonetic level makes selection more difficult (as with the Czech), similarity of meaning (with the French translation) produced no general increase in interference. (5) Finally, when both messages are in the same language and same voice, selection is based chiefly on transitional probabilities between words and its efficiency varies with the degree of contextual constraint within both the selected and irrelevant messages. This is the only condition in which a considerable number of overt intrusions from the irrelevant message is made.

These findings are relevant to the following problems: (1) Are both messages fully analyzed before one is selected to determine the responses? (2) If not, at what stage in the analysis is one of the two discarded? (3) What determines selection and switching between messages? How does this depend on the familiarity and phonetic structure of the languages and on the transitional probabilities between words?

(1) Analysis of irrelevant message. For the following reasons, it seems unlikely that both messages are always fully analyzed and that selection takes place only for the overt responses: (a) less than half the Ss recognized either the French translation or the Czech nonsense, although this would have added no more load to response or memory than noticing the male voice. Those who did identify these messages may have done so by switching to the irrelevant message.

— — —

(2) Stage at which selection is made. The question then arises: at what stage is one of the two messages rejected from further analysis? It does not seem possible to reject or filter out irrelevant messages which differ only in

verbal characteristics in the same efficient way as those which differ in general physical features.

— — —

If this early selection were possible between messages in the same voice but different languages, known and unknown languages should cause equal interference and both should be easier to reject than a message in the same language as the selected message. Neither of these predictions was confirmed by the results.

The results thus suggest that features of incoming messages are analyzed successively by the nervous system, starting with general physical features and proceeding to the identification of words and meaning, and that selection between messages in the same voice, intensity, and localization takes place during, rather than before or after, the analysis which results in the identification of their verbal content. It seems to be at this stage that the information-handling capacity becomes limited and can handle only one input at a time, either keeping to one message where possible, or switching between the two. Broadbent's suggestion that one may think of classes of words as constituting separate "input channels" which can be rejected, as such, is not supported by these results.

(3) Factors determining selection and switching between messages. What, then, determines selection and switching when both messages arrive on one input channel? The irrelevant messages seem to fall into two main classes: (a) those which the Ss potentially could identify; and (b) those whose verbal content they could never identify at all, because the language was unknown or the tape played backwards.

(a) When the irrelevant message was in a known foreign language or in English, the interference often took the form of making the Ss shift their attention to the wrong message and lose the correct message altogether for a time. The results with the statistical approximations suggest that the Ss repeat the correct message until its transitional probabilities fall to a low value. Differences in the competing messages do not affect the point at which they switch, but do affect their subsequent performance. Having switched, the Ss have two decisions to make: whether to repeat aloud what they hear, or to switch back. The instructions were to repeat as much as possible, rather than remaining silent when in doubt. This would encourage the Ss to make overt responses until they switched back, except when these were obvious errors, such as words in a different language.

We can now try to interpret these experiments and hypothesize what must be happening. To summarize Treisman's results once more, she found a graded effect on the ability of her subjects to reject an irrelevant message. When there was a distinct physical difference between relevant and irrelevant channels, subjects had no difficulty in shadowing one without being bothered by the other. When the messages had similar physical characteristics but belonged to different languages, they were much less successful. The better the subjects knew the irrelevant languages, the more it interfered. The most difficult task was to maintain shadowing one message when both were read in the same language and spoken with the same voice.

To explain these results, Treisman postulates an analytical mechanism that performs a series of tests on incoming messages. The first tests distinguish among the inputs on the basis of sensory or physical cues; later tests distinguish among syllabic patterns, specific sounds, individual words, and finally, grammatical structure and meaning. The sequence of tests can be thought of as a tree, with incoming sensory information starting at the bottom and working its way up to a unique end point, with tests at each spot where there is a choice of branches that might be taken. Moreover, Treisman suggests that the tests be flexible, so that if a particular word is expected, all the tests relevant to selecting that word might be prebiased or presensitized toward it. Thus, analysis is much simplified for items that are expected to occur.

If channels have physical distinctions, then at a very early stage of testing it will be possible to separate one from the other. This is done by attenuating the irrelevant channel so that it no longer interferes with the later testing procedure. Thus, words that appear on the irrelevant channel will be severely attenuated because they fail the physical test. If, however, a word on the irrelevant channel fits within the context of the material which has just been analyzed, it might very well be detected because the sensitization of each test toward the expected event would tend to cancel the effects of the attenuation of the irrelevant channel. Note, by the way, that by this model we ought to make mistakes, often claiming to have heard an item that was not actually presented. These false recognitions are a result of the lowered decision criteria for the tests relevant to expected events. Thus, although this presensitization makes detection of the correct event more likely, it also increases the likelihood that similar sounding items will pass the test incorrectly.

Treisman moves us one step further in the specification of the level at which attention becomes selective. She suggests that all incoming signals are analyzed to some extent by a sequence of operations. Signals are separated from one another by their physical features when that is possible and by their grammatical features when that becomes necessary. Grammatical information is used to bias or sensitize the criterion for identifying certain signals. Thus, in the middle of a sentence we might expect a certain grammatical class of words to occur, so we presensitize our analytical mechanisms for the possibility. This explains why we are sometimes able to pick out material which is presented in competing messages when that material appears to be relevant to the context to which we are primarily attending. The details of this procedure are left unexplained. Obviously it implies that all signals, whether thought to be relevant or irrelevant, must receive a good deal of analysis, if only so that they may be discarded with some certainty. The infrequent relevant signal from interfering channels would never get through the attention mechanism had it not received some identification before the final selection process took place.

AN ALTERNATIVE APPROACH

Our neat, pretty picture of an attention mechanism has disappeared. William James described how one stream of thought was separated from all possible ones. It appeared that this was an automatic process, requiring but little mental effort and resulting in a major simplification of duties for higher level processes. But now the story is not so simple. Evidently, we choose among incoming channels of information on the basis of rather complex analyses of the incoming signals. We had assumed that the purpose of selective attention was to allow a central mechanism to concentrate its efforts on analyzing and responding to one problem at a time. But now it appears that selection among alternative channels itself requires complex processing. What have we gained by the concept of a selective mechanism?

The main argument against Treisman's explanation concerns the complexity of the operations she proposes. Presumably, the selective nature of attention serves the purpose of reducing the amount of analysis that some central device must perform on incoming information by feeding it only one signal at a time. This concept is fine as long as the selection can be performed by looking for simple, physical differences among the signals. It is very easy to conceive of a system that separates a man's voice from a woman's or a voice on the left from one on the right. As soon as we are forced to use the meaning of signals to aid us in our selection, the problem becomes very complex. The meaning of the peculiar sound waveform that comprises a word cannot be determined without extensive analysis of the signal, an analysis that must use information stored in memory. At this point the whole purpose of a selective mechanism seems to disappear, for if we need to extract the meaning of all incoming signals to determine what to attend to, how does the selectivity help us?

There are two ways of answering this question while still retaining the notion of selective attention. The first is the proposal offered by Treisman. By attenuating some channels, she hopes to reduce the load placed on the central analyzing process while still allowing occasional signals on nonselected channels to sneak through when their meaning is relevant. The problem with this is simply that it is difficult to see how Treisman can have both a savings in the number of signals that must be analyzed (an attenuated signal, after all, acts like it is hardly there at all) and an analysis of all signals when it is convenient (the attenuated signal is still there, after all).

An alternative theory of selective attention requires us to move the selection mechanism back a bit. That is, suppose we admit that every incoming signal does indeed find its match in memory and receive a simple analysis for its meaning. Then, we let the selective attention mechanism take over from there. We still save some work because there is a lot more to understanding the meaning of the sequence of signals arriving on an information channel than simply looking up each one in memory. By this procedure, however, we have to assume that the way by which a sensory signal gets to memory is done automatically and by means of the sensory features of the signal alone. This has important implications for a theory of memory, as well as for the theory of attention and selection.

The general framework for this type of theory of attention was first stated in 1963 by the psychologists J. Anthony Deutsch and Diana Deutsch, then at Oxford, England (Deutsch and Deutsch, 1963). The Deutschs' theory can be elaborated, however, in a way not unrelated to the suggestion of Treisman (see Norman, 1968). Consider the scheme outlined in Fig. 2.

All signals arriving at sensory receptors pass through a stage of analysis performed by the early physiological processes. Then, the parameters extracted from these processes are used to determine where the representation of the sensory signal is stored. Thus, as shown in Fig. 2, all sensory signals excite their stored representation in memory. Now, at the same time, we assume that an analysis of previous signals is going on. This establishes a class of events deemed to be *pertinent* to the ongoing analysis. The set of pertinent items also excite their representation in memory. The item most highly excited by the combination of sensory and pertinence inputs is selected for further analysis (the shaded item in Fig. 2).

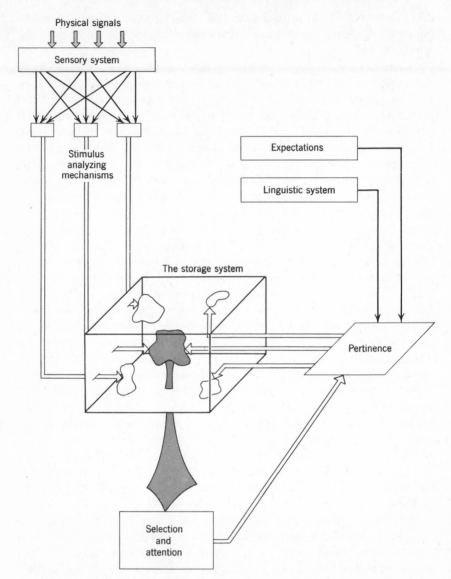

Fig. 2. The selection process. Both the physical inputs and the pertinence of information determine what will be selected for further processing. Physical inputs pass through the sensory system and stimulus analyzing mechanisms before exciting their representation in the storage system. Simultaneously, the analysis of previously encountered material, coupled with the history of expectations and the rules of perception, determine the class of events assumed to be most pertinent at the moment. That material which receives the greatest combined excitation is selected for further attention.

Given the selected item, the attention process now completes its analysis, adding the newly acquired information to what has come before and bringing the pertinence judgments up to date. This scheme is capable of describing the existing experimental data as well as the attenuation model of Treisman, especially if we allow physical cues to be included in the determination of the set of pertinent items.

Which model is preferable? At the moment the choice is somewhat arbitrary because critical experimental tests have not yet been performed. How different are these models? The main controversy concerns the level of processing at which the selection among channels takes place. One model places primary emphasis on selection by the use of physical cues, but with provisions for allowing important signals to be selected, regardless of physical characteristics. The other model suggests that selection takes place only after meaningful components of all sensory signals have been extracted. Both models require that the analysis of presently arriving signals is aided by the prior analysis of the context and expectations involved in the situation. Thus, although there are specific distinctions, the general features of both models are similar. The arguments are not as far apart as they might seem, as recent works by Morton (1969) and Neisser (1967) are able to demonstrate. These papers agree that analysis of incoming information is aided by prior analysis of the context and expectations involved in the situation. Sensory signals are involved in the activation of representations stored in memory (Morton calls them "logogens") and selection of important material occurs from the total impact of the actually occurring physical signal and the expectations and pertinence of the possible signals. In these models there is the implicit assumption (stated explicitly by Neisser) that "attention" describes the overall effect rather than being a specific selective process. Thus, it is possible that in the next few years the various dissimilar models of attention will discover that they are, in fact, quite compatible with one another; different models simply address different aspects of the problem.

The rest of this book is concerned with topics in perception and memory. These topics are intimately related to our study of attention and it is not possible to understand one without understanding the others. If some mechanism is able to assess the relative worth of different sensory messages, leaving one or a limited number for further processing, then it can do so only through an analysis which must include information stored in memory. We need information about the past in order to interpret the present. The interactions of sensory inputs with pattern recognition and memory are essential parts of human information processing.

Let us look now at the way we interpret incoming sensory information: the problem of pattern perception of that incoming information.

The attention mechanism cannot select intelligently among alternative channels of information unless it can first make a basic identification of the nature of the information. Suppose we hear several voices in the same ear. If we are to select one speaker, we must be able to extract from the complex acoustical waveform resulting from the combined voices, the features corresponding to each voice. This problem is one of pattern recognition and it has been studied more by specialists in computers, automata theory, and artificial intelligence than by psychologists. In the next chapter we review pattern recognition and the process of acquiring information.

SUGGESTED READINGS

The reader who wishes to learn more about attention should start by reading the complete versions of the papers discussed here. The task is simplified considerably, however, if the book by Ulric Neisser (1967) is used as a guide—Chapters 3, 4, and 8, in particular.

There is still considerable disagreement about the level at which the attention mechanism takes place. We have discussed some of this disagreement in the chapter. Amplification of Treisman's position has been presented in a paper by Treisman and Geffin (1967). An expansion of the opposing argument is provided in a paper by Norman (1968). The paper by John Morton (1969), although not directly concerned with the area of attention, is also highly relevant. The controversy has been brought out in the open by a discussion among Deutsch, Deutsch, Lindsay, and Treisman (1967). Some thoughts both relevant and irrelevant to the arguments are presented in a recent symposium on Attention and Performance, edited by A. F. Sanders (1967). Finally, a number of people are now writing books on the topic. Among the authors the reader should watch for are Donald Broadbent, Neville Moray, and Anne Treisman. (Be warned that the word "attention" has a number of different meanings in psychology. A book with the word "attention" in the title does not necessarily treat the same material covered in this chapter.)

The following journals contain most of the relevant literature:

American Journal of Psychology
Journal of the Acoustical Society of America (Sections 4 and 9)
Journal of Experimental Psychology
Perception and Psychophysics
Psychological Review
The Quarterly Journal of Experimental Psychology

3

The Acquisition of Information

ONE common view of human information processing suggests that the sense organs serve only as transducers, changing physical energy to some physiological representation. An attention mechanism then selects interesting aspects of the physiological image of the world for further processing by a central system. According to this viewpoint, the sensory system is something like a television channel, conveying information about the environment by encoding the visual and acoustical information received in as complete and undistorted a fashion as possible. This description is wrong.

STIMULUS ANALYZING MECHANISMS

The picture that has emerged from the results of an increasingly large number of experiments in psychology, physiology, neurology, and the communication sciences implies that the nervous system performs substantial alterations of the physical image received by the sense organs. These transformations extract information about color, enhance contours, determine size and direction of movement of visual images, extract the pitch and loudness of acoustical images, and determine the spatial and temporal relationships of visual and acoustical signals. These transformations are of great use to the nervous system because they simplify tremendously the information that must be transmitted to higher level analyzing systems. This, in turn, simplifies the job of analyzing the sensory inputs. Transformations waste information, however, for aspects of the

37

signal that are combined with one another at one level of processing cannot be separated at higher levels.

Thus, information about incoming signals is abstracted by a number of different analyzing mechanisms. As this information is processed by the nervous system, the outputs of the analyzers may be successively combined, forming a hierarchical process whereby the outputs of one level of analyzers are analyzed by yet another. Presumably the types of analyzers are limited, but the ways in which they can be combined are not.

It is not yet possible to determine how stimulus recognition is accomplished. It is possible, however, to review a number of possible mechanisms and determine what demands and implications they have for the processes of attention and memory. In this chapter the primary emphasis is on the *psychology* of perception. We start where the physiologists leave off, trying to determine how humans work with and manipulate the messages sent over the sensory pathways. The basic problem is to determine how we match the complex sensory waveforms with material which is stored in memory.

The problem can be illustrated most easily by an analysis of speech. The acoustical waveform of speech is very complicated. Yet we are able to transform this waveform into meaningful messages at a very rapid rate. This transformation requires us to decompose the speech into its basic linguistic components, match what we hear to information which is already stored in long-term memory, and perform the necessary syntactic and semantic analysis in order to determine the meaning of the message. Several stages of processing are necessary in doing this analysis. First we must transform the sensory waveforms into some physiological representation. Then, in order to interpret the incoming sensory message, we must get both it and the material stored in memory into the same type of physiological coding. Even this obvious step is extremely difficult. Spoken words have to reduce to a common format which is independent of accents and peculiarities of the individual speaker. Indeed, visually presented words must end up in a similar format to auditorally presented words, for we make no distinction in meaning based on the difference between speaking and writing.

Bypassing, for the moment, the matching of the sensory input to material stored in memory, we still have to contend with the problem of attaching the proper meaning to the input. In recent years there has been a good deal of speculation and argumentation about the nature of this operation. The field of contention seems to have broken down into two opposing viewpoints (with many dissenting opinions within each camp): one assumes that the analysis proceeds by attempting to recreate the sensory signal, matching the synthesized version with the actual input; and the other assumes that a passive recognition of the input is sufficient. We shall review some of the arguments for both points of view in this chapter.

One of the early discussions of the general nature of stimulus analyzing mechanisms and the implications such mechanisms have on perception and attention was presented by the English psychologist N. Stuart Sutherland at a symposium on thought processes held in 1958. Sutherland argued that much of the limitations on performance studied in the literature on attention can be explained by assuming that there are a few very general analyzing mechanisms which can be programmed to operate in a very flexible manner. When a particular mechanism is set to perform one task, it cannot do other tasks: hence, the limitation on operations that can be performed simultaneously. Basically, Sutherland suggested that a set of very specific stimulus analyzing mechanisms extracted important parameters from sensory events—parameters such as the direction or movement of lines, of color, and of boundaries—followed by a set of very general purpose mechanisms which could be connected (or instructed to operate) in a variety of ways. Thus, specific analyzers might be used in different ways to categorize sensory information. Although the analyzers would be located at specific sense organs, the general mechanisms might be applied to a variety of problems and sensory modalities. By this scheme, there would occasionally be competition for specific analyzing mechanisms and a particular configuration of the general purpose mechanism might be ill-suited for a new task. These competitions and specificities could provide a rationale for the observations from studies of attention that humans have a limited capacity to deal with incoming information. Although the nervous system is quite capable of performing a large variety of operations, if these were to require different interconnections or instructions of a limited set of general mechanisms, it would not be capable of performing these operations in several different ways at once.

Sutherland argues his case from two sources: economy and experimental evidence on animal discrimination experiments. Today there is more physiological evidence, the two most important papers being descriptions of specific pattern detection devices in the frog (Lettvin, Maturana, McCulloch, and Pitts, 1959) and specialized receptors in the visual cortex of the cat (Hubel and Wiesel, 1959, 1962). The frog has a very specific detection system, prewired to notice small, black objects (bugs) and other phenomenon relevant to its life. The cat is more general, having specific neural cells for analyzing line segments, orientation, and movement. The work on the cat fits very nicely into the scheme outlined by Sutherland: a set of very special analyzing mechanisms extracts basic features from the visual image. However, general purpose programming devices then operate to organize and interpret the special features according to learned rules.

The main disagreement about pattern recognition starts at this point. Impressed by the powerful types of detectors for very specific events which have been uncovered by recent physiological research, a number of people suggest that all pattern recognition is done this way. That is, for each specific pattern that we are able to classify, there is a specific network of neurons that identifies whenever that pattern occurs in the environment. At the present time, in the absence of evidence one way or the other, the only argument against this notion is the one of economy already advanced by Sutherland. The number of possible patterns, combinations of patterns, and new viewing angles (and perspectives and distortions) lead to a staggering amount of complexity in the neural networks required to do the task. Moreover, it is not clear that any finite network could ever suffice, for there are truly an infinite number of ways we can see well-known objects (just as there are an infinite number of sentences we can construct from well-known words).

The opposing viewpoint suggests that we recognize patterns by rules. That is, a set of rather general purpose operations examine the set of features extracted by the basic physiological analyzers and classify patterns, more by synthesizing them anew than by any other procedure.

One way of illustrating the distinction between these techniques is to consider the difference between these two questions which might be asked by the pattern recognition device of the incoming signal:

1. Which classification of patterns (of the many that I have learned) does that represent?

2. What do I have to do to one of my previously learned patterns to make it look like that?

The differences between these two questions are subtle, but so are the issues: One statement (1) classifies the incoming signals; the other (2) actively matches it.

THE IMPORTANCE OF CONTEXT

Sutherland's descriptions represent an early, sophisticated statement of a passive system of pattern recognition. Once the various mechanisms have been set up, incoming sensory signals go through a sequence of fixed neurological processes and, *voila!*, come out identified, labeled, and tagged. The problem with such a system is that our interpretation of sensory signals depends upon the whole environment in which they are imbedded. Thus, ambiguous perceptions get interpreted in completely unambiguous ways, depending upon the context surrounding them. All of us must have had the experience of misreading a word or failing to see an indistinct or distant object. Yet, when told what the word or object really was, we looked again and suddenly it was clear and distinct: why did we have trouble in the first place? [1] Evidently we are able to change the rules of pattern recognition as we go along, dynamically adjusting to our expectations. Sutherland's model, written in 1958 before much of the modern work on pattern recognition, is quite capable of incorporating dynamic flexibility. The most important feature of his description, the stimulus analyzing mechanisms, should remain unchanged—they are needed by most modern theories. The control center must increase substantially in size and power, however, for it must readjust the manner in which it uses the outputs of stimulus analyzers as a function of how it interprets the total situation which it is attempting to analyze.

Contextual information is of great importance in perceptual processing. The average skilled reader, for example, is able to process between 300 to 600 words each minute.[2] In order to do this, he must be able to identify as many as 10 words and, presumably, 50 to 70 letters, each second. This is faster than the recognition process can operate on isolated letters or words. This high rate is illusory, however, because grammatical text has many constraints on it. From any point of view, language is highly redundant. Our language habits impose severe restraints on the possible and likely sequences of letters that can appear within a word, the sequence of words that can appear in any sentence, and the way ideas are introduced on a page. It is possible to take advantage of all these aspects of language so that, in order to read, only a little information need be

[1] This phenomenon is so dramatic that it has been used by John Morton at a public lecture in England. He played a recorded song (from a performance by the Beatles) to his audience and asked them to identify the words. They failed. Then he flashed the words on a screen and played the recording again. This time the words were "heard" distinctly.

[2] In this discussion we ignore the performance obtained with special speed-reading techniques. Although these techniques apparently allow individuals to "read" material at rates measured in the thousands and tens of thousands of words per minute, this remarkable speed need not be primarily a result of an increased rate of processing individual words. The speed reader can improve his rate by taking full advantage of the redundancy of the written language, eliminating wasted eye movements (such as regressions), and skipping much irrelevant material. In any event, we have enough trouble explaining the performance of the normal reader.

extracted from individual letters or words. In fact, most of the letters and many of the words in text can be skipped without any loss in intelligibility.

These statements imply that our pattern recognition devices need not actually operate completely on all material fed to them. If they are able to take advantage of the context, they need only monitor the inputs and signal when something unexpected happens. Monitoring a signal to see if it is one of a few limited possibilities is a much simpler task than studying it to determine exactly which of the many alternatives it is. But this technique requires an intimate link between the operations of the pattern recognition device and the operations of determining the meaning of the material which is being analyzed.

Now we begin to see why there are so many arguments in the literature about passive versus active pattern recognition devices. The engineer would like to have a machine that pieces together each individual part of the pattern to determine which word it represents. There is no logical reason why this could not be done. Certainly the printed and spoken words are well-defined and the rules of spelling and pronunciation well-documented. Why do we need anything more than a simple device for pattern recognition? The need for a different type of device becomes apparent when we realize that human recognition of speech and reading occurs faster than it ought to and that missing words, errors in speech, printing, or grammar, and high noise levels seem to have little effect on our ability to understand verbal matter.

READING AND SPEECH RECOGNITION

A simple experiment can illustrate many of these points. Try to read material which is held upside down. (It is better to start with highly redundant material, such as a light novel or a child's book, rather than something technical.) Practice reading for a while, perhaps as much as an hour. As you practice, you will note a dramatic increase in your rate of reading. At first you will have trouble with individual letters, but soon you will ignore the letters and read words, then finally, whole phrases. As you read in this unusual way you are able to notice habits of which you were unaware in normal reading. You don't see all of a word: you tend to guess. You find yourself reading long phrases quite rapidly, but only because you knew it was likely to have occurred in the context of the passage. The process is quite automatic and not nearly so conscious and deliberate as this description would imply. In fact, the way to discover what you are doing is to make a mistake: realize that those last few words don't make sense in the context of the sentence, or that the ending "ing" just doesn't belong to the word you read. Then, once the mistake is made, it is often possible to go back and recreate what must have happened. (Some further descriptions of this process are provided by Kolers, in press.)

Reading upside down is a convenient way of slowing down the normal process so that we can introspect about our operations. It is a rather convincing demonstration of the complexity of normal reading and the efficient way in which we use clues to avoid having to process every aspect of the printed page.

Some of the same points can also be illustrated by speeding up the normal process. Read a page of text while timing yourself. Then read it two more times, first very slowly—word by word—then once more, moderately slowly. Now read the entire passage as rapidly as you can, timing your rate of reading. You should be able to double your reading speed this way. Now read the passage once more, again while timing yourself. You should still be improving, but the last reading is approaching the speed reached by speed-reading techniques, although you probably move your eyes very inefficiently. (Obviously, this is not the technique used by speed readers, although it is not a bad training method.) Note that you did not read the material as much as you confirmed it; the prior knowledge of the contents of the material was essential to the success of the trial.

DECISION UNITS

The perception of printed words has much in common with the perception of speech. A good deal of the work on pattern recognition devices has dealt with speech recognition. We can recognize speech under very poor conditions; the speech waveform may be distorted, mixed with noise, fragmented, and be, in general, a very poor representation of the sounds which actually were spoken by the talker. In speech recognition we do several things that have not usually been considered necessary for pattern recognition. First, we use the habits of the speaker to help decode his words. We always do better at understanding speech after we have listened to the speaker for a while. This implies that we change the characteristics of our analyzing mechanisms to match the characteristics of the speaker. Second, we use the grammar of language to help us. We do better at recognizing material when the number of possible words is limited, but adding grammatical constraints improves our performance even more. Use of these rules lets us reject possibilities which do not fit into the rule. Note that general linguistic rules are required, not a dictionary of possibilities. Systems which store all possible words (in the case of speech), or all possible combinations of two words, or of three words, and so on, hoping to decode speech by matching each set of physical signals against a possible stored representation are doomed to failure, if only because the size of the dictionary they must maintain will increase without limit. There is no grammatical rule which limits the size of sentences. Moreover, almost every sentence we hear, read, or speak is novel and differs in some way from all other sentences we have previously encountered. A pattern recognition device which hopes to take advantage of the statistics of spoken speech is going to have trouble with all these unique arrangements.

Third, we do not recognize speech at the same time as we hear it. Rather, we tend to hang back, delaying the decoding process for a syllable or two, waiting to get more information about the signal. This tactic of delay is very important and common. As we discussed in Chapter 2, the skilled receiver of Morse Code or the stenographer writes down the message with a rather large delay after its actual reception. When we read aloud or type (skillfully), our eyes examine the manuscript quite far in advance of the part that we actually speak or type. Although the examples are numerous, few theories or devices for pattern recognition seem to use this principle (with the exception of the selections we shall examine here).

These properties of human performance are stressed in the next selection, a paper by George Miller. Miller believes that artificial pattern recognition devices are probably using the wrong information for their decisions. He suggests that automatic speech recognizers could learn from the techniques used by humans.

THE PERCEPTION OF SPEECH *

GEORGE A. MILLER

It is often assumed that when we are listening to speech we are making phonetic decisions, phonemic decisions, syntactic decisions, semantic decisions—

* George A. Miller. Decision units in the perception of speech. *IRE Transactions on Information Theory*, 1962, IT-8, 81–83. Copyright 1962 by The Institute of Radio Engineering (now called the Institute of Electrical and Electronics Engineers, Inc.). With permission of the author and the Institute of Electrical and Electronics Engineers.

all more or less simultaneously. Since the decision units involved in these hypothetical decisions are hierarchically related, one might expect that decisions would be made first at the lowest level, then the outcome would provide a basis for decisions at the next higher level, etc. No doubt this approach is reasonable and could be made the basis for a device to recognize speech, but there are several reasons for doubting if it describes the way people naturally operate. One of the strongest criticisms is a subjective one: Phenomenologically, it seems that the larger, more meaningful decisions are made first, and that we pursue the details only so far as they are necessary to serve our immediate purposes. The ancient belief that perceptual wholes are compounded by associating independent elements of sensation has a very poor reputation among modern psychologists, and any attempt to give priority to the molecular processes is likely to encounter considerable scepticism.

But let us pursue this model a bit further. If the small details of input are discriminated first, how is it possible to take advantage of the redundancy of the message? Presumably, the sequence of preceding decisions must be stored and used to limit the set of alternatives among which the next decision is to be made. Such a Markovian mechanism, however, would lead to compound errors. Once a mistake occurs, the incorrect context so created tends to cause further mistakes until the process of recognition becomes stalled. A reasonable answer to this objection, however, is that we must regard the decisions reached at the lower levels as tentative and subject to revision pending the outcome of decisions made at some higher, more molar level. Once this tentative character is admitted, of course, it becomes necessary to continue storing the original input until the molar decisions have been reached.

However, if complete storage is necessary even after the lower-level decisions have been tentatively reached why bother to make the lower-level decisions first? Why not store the message until enough of it is on hand to support a higher-level decision, then make a decision for all levels simultaneously?

One advantage of a delayed-decision strategy is that the decision rate is reduced. Consider the rates we must cope with: In order to comprehend messages spoken at 150 words/minutes, we would presumably have to make about a dozen phonemic decisions every second, and perhaps 100 phonetic decisions. To say that people can make decisions at such rates is to extend the concept well beyond its usual psychological range. Many psychologists have measured the time required to make a decision among several alternatives; reaction times in the neighborhood of 0.2 to 0.5 seconds are commonly obtained. The exact value, of course, depends upon the exact conditions of measurement. An important point for the present argument, however, is that for highly practiced subjects the time required to make a choice reaction may *not* increase as a function of the number of alternatives that can occur (Mowbray, 1960). The time required to decide between two alternatives is effectively the same as that required for 30 alternatives. This fact is important for the present discussion, since it means that a single delayed decision would require far less time than would a series of immediate decisions. Our limited decision rate imposes a much stronger constraint on our channel capacity than does our limited ability to discriminate accurately among many alternatives.

Of course, the rates that psychologists have measured have generally been close to the maximum. It seems plausible that ordinary conversation would put less strain on us. Perhaps we make about one decision per second in ordinary listening. If we accept this as a rough estimate, it suggests that the phrase— usually about two or three words at a time—is probably the natural decision unit for speech.

Miller, Heise, and Lichten (1951) reported that words spoken in the context of a sentence can be identified more accurately than the same words spoken in isolation, but in haphazard order. This result supports the assumption that decisions about smaller units can be more accurate when they occur in a re- dundant context. But how do listeners take advantage of this redundancy? Miller, Heise, and Lichten attributed the superior intelligibility to the fact that the sentence context reduces the number of alternative words among which a listener must decide. "The effect of the sentence is comparable," they wrote, "to the effect of a restricted vocabulary, although the degree of restriction is harder to estimate. When the talker begins a sentence, 'Apples grow on . . . ,' the range of possible continuations is sharply restricted. This restriction makes the discrimination easier and lowers the threshold of intelligibility."

This explanation may be logically correct, but it carries an implication that listeners make successive decisions about words while they are listening to sentences. In view of the present argument, however, we question whether a decision could be made about word N fast enough to limit the alternatives con- sidered for word $N + 1$.

In order to test whether words heard in sentences are more intelligible because the number of alternative words is reduced or because sentences permit a delayed decision, an experiment was conducted that held the num- ber of alternatives constant but varied the sequential properties of the test lists. A vocabulary of 25 monosyllabic English words was selected and or- ganized into five subvocabularies of five words each, as shown in Table 1. Intelligibility tests were conducted at several signal-to-noise ratios with each of the five subvocabularies and with the entire vocabulary of 25 words. In these tests a list of 100 consecutive words was read at a rate of about 1.5 words/sec. Listeners repeated what they heard into a dictating machine. In order to maintain synchrony, the talker paused slightly after every fifth word.

It was found, as anticipated, that a word is more often heard correctly when the listener expects it as one of five alternatives than when he expects it as one of 25. The more interesting conditions, however, were the following:

Table 1   Five Subvocabularies Used to Explore the Perceptual Effects of Grammatical Content

1	2	3	4	5
Don	Brought	His	Black	Bread
He	Has	More	Cheap	Sheep
Red	Left	No	Good	Shoes
Slim	Loves	Some	Wet	Socks
Who	Took	The	Wrong	Things

One type of test list was constructed by randomly choosing the first word from subvocabulary 1, the second from subvocabulary 2, the third from 3, the fourth from 4, the fifth from 5, the sixth from 1 again, etc. The reader should verify for himself that the result of this procedure is to generate English sentences: "Slim loves more wet sheep" and "He has the wrong socks" are typical examples. Then, to contrast with the sentences, test lists consisting of pseudo-sentences were formed by selecting the words in reverse order: "Sheep wet more loves slim" and "Socks wrong the has he" illustrate the result obtained here.

The important feature of test lists constructed in this manner is that each successive word is one of five possibilities—the number of alternatives is the same—but in one case a listener can use his grammatical habits to form longer units, whereas in the other case grammar is no help and he must make an immediate decision about each word as it occurs.

The results of these tests are plotted in Fig. 1. The tests with sentences and

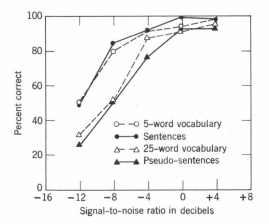

Fig. 1. Grammatical context improves intelligibility, but ungrammatical context does not—even though the number of alternative words that could occur was the same in both cases.

with the 5-word vocabularies gave the same results, so the experiment verifies the claim that the sentence context effectively reduces the number of alternatives from 25 to 5. However, pseudo-sentences, which also involved five alternatives, gave the same function—perhaps slightly lower—as did the tests with a 25-word vocabulary. The listeners were unable to take advantage of the reduced number of alternatives in the pseudo-sentences—presumably because they could not shift rapidly enough from one subvocabulary to the next when the shifts occurred in a nongrammatical order—and so they treated each word as if it could have been any one of the 25 in the total vocabulary.

It should be noted that the test lists were read at a relatively rapid pace and without significant pauses. When the lists were read at a rate of one word every two seconds, pseudo-sentences were heard just as well as were the sentences or the tests using 5-word vocabularies. Indeed, even when the pseudo-sentences were read at regular conversational speeds, but with a 10 second pause between successive pseudo-sentences, they were heard almost as well as are the 5-word tests. In order to demonstrate that the pseudo-sentences were more difficult than grammatical sentences, it was necessary to read them rapidly and continuously so that delayed decisions were truly impossible.

We can describe this experiment in slightly different terms, as follows: The basic *vocabulary* from which the test lists were constructed was a set of 25^5 sequences of five words. For some lists, subvocabularies consisting of 5^5 alternative sequences were selected. When these subvocabularies were selected by reducing the number of different words that could occur in the tests, or by making the sequences conform to grammatical rules, the listener's task was easier. But when the subvocabulary consisted of 5^5 alternative sequences selected by nongrammatical rules, the listener was not able to take advantage of it.

When the experiment is described in this way, the result seems wholly in line with what one might expect on the basis of the well-established principal that smaller vocabularies make easier listening. The important thing to notice, however, is that 5^5 is a large vocabulary and five syllables is a long delay. If we accept this principle in general we shall be faced with a much larger dictionary of decision units than our usual dictionaries would lead us to expect.

An engineer hoping to build devices that will recognize speech has a right to be discouraged with this result. His machines are much better at lightning fast decisions among relatively few alternatives, whereas people are better at making slow decisions about relatively large amounts of information. Presumably there is quite a lot of rapid, parallel processing going on in the brain, even though the decision mechanism itself seems to be the sluggish serial device we have already described.

There is no *a priori* reason to insist that recognition devices must work on the same principle as does the human being. It should be born in mind, however, that speech is uttered for human ears. If people do in fact follow a strategy of delayed-decisions in listening to the on-going flow of speech, then there is no guarantee that a speech signal must always contain the kind of information needed to support a sequence of immediate decisions. It may yet prove necessary to use our perceptual and grammatical knowledge, before we succeed in building reliable speech recognizers.

Miller elegantly illustrates that we use grammatical information obtained from the structure of a sentence to improve our perception of the individual words of that sentence. The grammatical information improves performance simply because it limits the number of alternative words we must consider when trying to understand speech. Miller argues, however, that humans normally cannot make decisions as rapidly as their performance in perceiving sentences would imply; hence, he suggests that we hang back, postponing interpretation of individual sounds until a reasonable sample has been assembled.

ANALYSIS BY SYNTHESIS

Miller's plea that automatic devices for speech recognition should not rely entirely on acoustical analysis but must also include information about language structure has not been entirely unheeded. In the very same issue of the journal that contained Miller's article, Morris Halle and Kenneth Stevens present a model of speech recognition that incorporates a good deal of linguistic information into the decision process. That the two articles should appear together is not entirely a coincidence. At the time the articles were written, Miller, Halle, and Stevens all worked in the amorphous community of scholars in Cambridge, Massachusetts: Miller at Harvard University and Halle and Stevens at the Massachusetts Institute of Technology. It is not clear how much the work of one influenced the work of the other, but it is clear that a whole new discipline of linguistic analysis had been in progress in Cambridge since the mid 1950's, involving psychologists, acousticians, linguists, and electrical engineers.

The papers of Miller and of Halle and Stevens are in violent disagreement about one aspect of linguistic processing: the speed at which it takes place. Miller argues that it proceeds slowly, with major decisions delayed until several syllables or words have been received. Halle and Stevens represent a different point of view. They suggest that humans interpret sounds by trying to generate them: if the self-generated utterance matches what has been heard, then obviously they must know what linguistic unit it represents. This procedure will not work, however, without extremely rapid generation of guesses, for the match of what is hypothesized to what is received must occur while the sound is still present. Before we get further into this area of controversy, however, let us examine the model put forth by Halle and Stevens.[3]

SPEECH RECOGNITION: A MODEL *

MORRIS HALLE and KENNETH STEVENS

The fundamental problem in pattern recognition is the search for a *recognition function* that will appropriately pair *signals* and *messages*. The input to the recognizer generally consists of measured physical quantities characterizing each signal to be recognized, while at the output of the recognizer each input signal is assigned to one of a number of categories which constitute the messages. Thus, for instance, in machine translation, the signals are sentences in one language and the messages are sentences in another language. In the automatic recognition of handwriting, the signal is a two-dimensional curve and the message a sequence of letters in a standard alphabet. Similarly, research on automatic speech recognition aims at discovering a recognition function that relates acoustic signals produced by the human vocal tract in speaking to messages consisting of strings of symbols, the phonemes. Such a recognition function is the inverse of a function that describes the production of speech, *i.e.*, the transformation of a discrete phoneme sequence into an acoustic signal.

This paper proposes a recognition model in which mapping from signal to message space is accomplished largely through an active or feedback process. Patterns are generated internally in the analyzer according to a flexible or adaptable sequence of instructions until a best match with the input

[3] A phoneme is the smallest unit of speech sounds that serves to distinguish two utterances which differ in meaning. The initial sounds of the words "pin" and "bin" represent different phonemes; the two "p" sounds of the word "pop," although sounding different, are the same phoneme. The utterances of any language can be characterized by a set of a few dozen phonemes.

* M. Halle and K. Stevens. Speech recognition: A model and a program for research. *IRE Transactions on Information Theory*, 1962, IT-8, 155–159. Copyright 1962 by The Institute of Radio Engineering (now called the Institute of Electrical and Electronics Engineers, Inc.). With permission of the authors and the Institute of Electrical and Electronics Engineers.

signal is obtained. Since the analysis is achieved through active internal synthesis of comparison signals, the procedure has been called "analysis by synthesis."

THE PROCESS OF SPEECH PRODUCTION

In line with the traditional account of speech production, we shall assume that the speaker has stored in his memory a table of all the phonemes and their actualizations. This table lists the different vocal-tract configurations or gestures that are associated with each phoneme and the conditions under which each is to be used. In producing an utterance the speaker looks up, as it were, in the table the individual phonemes and then instructs his vocal tract to assume in succession the configurations or gestures corresponding to the phonemes.

The shape of man's vocal tract is not controlled as a single unit; rather, separate control is exercised over various gross structures in the tract, e.g., the lip opening, position of velum, tongue position, and vocal-cord vibration. The changing configurations of the vocal tract must, therefore, be specified in terms of parameters describing the behavior of these quasi-independent structures. These parameters will be called *phonetic parameters*.

Since the vocal tract does not utilize the same amount of time for actualizing each phoneme (e.g., the vowel in *bit* is considerably shorter than that in *beat*), it must be assumed that stored in the speaker's memory there is also a schedule that determines the time at which the vocal tract moves from one configuration to the next, i.e., the time at which one or more phonetic parameters change in value. The timing will evidently differ depending on the speed of utterance—it will be slower for slower speech and faster for faster speech.

— — —

REDUCTION OF THE CONTINUOUS SIGNAL TO A MESSAGE CONSISTING OF DISCRETE SYMBOLS; THE SEGMENTATION PROBLEM

The analysis procedure that has enjoyed the widest acceptance postulates that the listener first segments the utterance and then identifies the individual segments with particular phonemes. No analysis scheme based on this principle has ever been successfully implemented. This failure is understandable in the light of the preceding account of speech production, where it was observed that segments of an utterance do not in general stand in a one-to-one relation with the phonemes. The problem, therefore, is to devise a procedure which will transform the continuously-changing speech signal into a discrete output without depending crucially on segmentation.

A simple procedure of this type restricts the input to stretches of sound separated from adjacent stretches by silence. The input signals could, for example, correspond to isolated words, or they could be longer utterances. Perhaps the crudest device capable of transforming such an input into phoneme sequences would be a "dictionary" in which the inputs are entered as intensity-frequency-time patterns and each entry is provided with its phonemic representation. The segment under analysis is compared with each entry in the dictionary, the one most closely resembling the input determined, and its phonemic transcription printed out.

The size of the dictionary in such an analyzer increases very rapidly with the number of admissible outputs, since a given phoneme sequence can give rise to a large number of distinct acoustic outputs. In a device whose capabilities would even remotely approach those of a normal human listener, the size of the dictionary would, therefore, be so large as to rule out this approach.

The need for a large dictionary can be overcome if the principles of construction of the dictionary entries are known. It is then possible to store in the "permanent memory" of the analyzer only the rules for speech production discussed in the previous section. In this model the dictionary is replaced by *generative rules* which can synthesize signals in response to instructions consisting of sequences of phonemes. Analysis is now accomplished by supplying the generative rules with all possible phoneme sequences, systematically running through all one-phoneme sequences, two-phoneme sequences, etc. The internally generated signal which provides the best match with the input signal then identifies the required phoneme sequence. While this model does not place excessive demands on the size of the memory, a very long time is required to achieve positive identification.

The necessity of synthesizing a large number of comparison signals can be eliminated by a *preliminary analysis* which excludes from consideration all but a very small subset of the items which can be produced by the generative rules. The preliminary analysis would no doubt include various transformations which have been found useful in speech analysis, such as segmentation within the utterance according to the type of vocal-tract excitation and tentative identification of segments by special attributes of the signal. Once a list of possible phoneme sequences is established from the preliminary analysis, then the internal signal synthesizer proceeds to generate signals corresponding to each of these sequences.

The analysis procedure can be refined still further by including a *control* component to dictate the order in which comparison signals are to be generated. This control is guided not only by the results of the preliminary analysis but also by quantitative measures of the goodness of fit achieved for comparison signals that have already been synthesized, statistical information concerning the admissible phoneme sequences, and other data that may have been obtained from preceding analyses. This information is utilized by the control component to formulate strategies that would achieve convergence to the required result with as small a number of trials as possible.

It seems to us that an automatic speech recognition scheme capable of processing any but the most trivial classes of utterances must incorporate all of the features discussed above—the input signal must be matched against a comparison signal; a set of generative rules must be stored within the machine; preliminary analysis must be performed; and a strategy must be included to control the order in which internal comparison signals are to be generated.

— — —

When signals generated by a different talker are presented, the strategy must be able to modify this group of instructions automatically after sufficient data on that talker's speech have been accumulated. The analysis-by-synthesis procedure has the property, therefore, that its strategy is potentially able to adapt to the characteristics of different talkers.

SUMMARY OF MODEL FOR SPEECH RECOGNITION

The complete model for speech recognition discussed here takes the form shown in Fig. 2. The input signal is first processed by a peripheral unit such as a spectrum analyzer. It then undergoes reduction in two analysis-by-synthesis

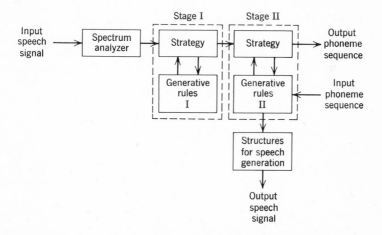

Fig. 2. Block diagram of two-stage scheme for speech processing. Following processing by a spectrum analyzer, the input speech signal is reduced in Stage I to a set of quasi-continuous phonetic parameters, which are processed in Stage II to yield an output phoneme sequence. An analysis-by-synthesis procedure is used for processing the signal at each stage. The heavy lines indicate the operations that are involved in generating a speech signal from a phoneme sequence.

loops, and the phoneme sequence appears at the right. In order to simplify the diagram, the group of components performing the functions of storage, preliminary analysis, comparison, and control have been combined in a single block labeled *strategy*.

The procedure depicted here is suitable only for the recognition of sequences of uncorrelated symbols, such as those that control the generation of nonsense syllables. If the speech material to be recognized consists of words, phrases, or continuous text, then the output of the present analysis scheme would have to be processed further to take account of the constraints imposed by the morphological and syntactic structure of the language.

The final analysis stage of Fig. 2 includes, of course, the generative rules for transforming phoneme sequences into phonetic parameters. These are precisely the rules that must be invoked in the production of speech. During speech production the output from these stored rules can be connected directly to the speech mechanism, while the input to the rules is the phoneme sequence to be generated. Addition of peripheral speech-generating structures to Fig. 2 then creates a model that is capable of both speech recognition and speech production. The same calculations are made in the second set of generative rules (and in the generative rules at possible higher levels of analysis) whether speech is being received or generated. It is worthwhile observing that during the recognition process phonetic parameters are merely calculated by the "generative rules II" and direct activation of the speech structures is nowhere required.

For the recognition of continuous speech it may not always be necessary to have recourse to analysis-by-synthesis procedures. A rough preliminary analysis at each of the stages in Fig. 2 may often be all that is required— ambiguities as a result of imprecise analysis at these early stages can be resolved in later stages on the basis of knowledge of the constraints at the morphological, syntactic, and semantic levels.

A strong point of Halle and Stevens' argument is that we use the same mechanism to generate speech as to perceive it. In this way they achieve economy in the mechanisms necessary for grammatical understanding and production. Note that there is no need for actual motor movements to occur in the synthesis progress: the hypothesis that speech perception involves a form of synthesis does not require that the listener actually say anything, not even to himself.

What can we say about the difference between the rate of analysis postulated by the delayed analysis of Miller and the analysis by synthesis of Halle and Stevens (or the very similar "motor" theory of perception: Liberman *et al*, 1967). Miller has argued that the decision rate required by the analysis by synthesis technique is too fast. On the other hand, we know from the experiments on attention that subjects doing phonemic shadowing can repeat a message with only a very slight delay between hearing a sound and speaking it (see Fant, 1967). If this is so, where is the long delay postulated by Miller? Let us postpone the question once more and look at another view of speech perception.

The main differences among models of speech perception are concerned with the way the incoming sensory signal is recognized. In particular, the schemes suggested by the models of attention in Chapter 2 and Sutherland's work discussed in this chapter imply a passive device by which the decoding of the speech waveform proceeds automatically through a series of stimulus analyzing networks, finally ending up by exciting specific locations of memory. The manner in which memory gets activated is determined entirely by the physical features of the speech signals. At first glance, this appears to be quite different than the procedure proposed by proponents of active models.

The active models, represented primarily by the analysis by synthesis scheme of Halle and Stevens and the motor theory of speech perception by workers at the Haskins Laboratory in New York (for example, Liberman, Cooper, Harris, MacNeilage, and M. Studdert-Kennedy, 1967), involve comparisons of the input sounds, acoustic representations, or methods of articulatory coding with internally generated signals. The difference between the input and the self-generated signal is used to correct the internal signal until a satisfactory match is made. Thus, by this model, we act as if we are creating the speech ourselves, recognizing the speech input only when what we generate matches what we hear.

The main objections to a passive analysis come from the lack of physical specificity of the speech waveform. Although it might appear obvious that the physical sounds uniquely determine the perceived words, the obviousness disappears when one tries to discover the physical correlates of sounds. For one thing, even the boundaries between words are ambiguous. For another, different physical signals sometimes sound similar and the same signals sometimes sound different. The difficulty becomes even more apparent when one listens to a foreign language for the first time. The speakers all appear to be going remarkably fast and, rather than uttering a sequence of separate words, there appears to be only one continuous flow of sound. The active models try to circumvent these difficulties by substituting a matching process. The main criticism aimed at these models is that their success depends very strongly upon the nature of the first guess, for otherwise the matching process might not keep up with the speech. When words are heard in the context of a sentence or story, the guess about each new word is tightly limited by the context. But then, how do we hear words in isolation?

DO THE MODELS DIFFER?

A detailed analysis of these different models indicates that they might not be so different after all. All models indicate the extreme importance of grammatical context on the perception of spoken words. Miller demonstrates this by the decreased perception of the same words in noise when they are not part of grammatical sentences. Halle and Stevens explicitly allow for the operation of linguistic rules to help in generating their comparison samples, and they suggest that only a rough analysis may be necessary at the acoustic level, with problems being resolved by constraints at the morphological, syntactic, and semantic levels. Finally, the models from the attention literature such as those of Morton and Norman (see Fig. 2 of Chapter 2) presensitize their basic analytical units according to expectations about spoken utterances based on the linguistic analysis of what has already been perceived.

Since all three viewpoints agree that complete speech recognition cannot be performed without complete linguistic analysis, there is no conflict among the ideas at this level. The main discrepancy appears to be between the passive decoding of sounds on the one hand and the active matching process of phoneme recognition on the other. In this aspect it would seem that the requirements of linguistic considerations—the active system—are in conflict with requirements of the results of studies in attention—the passive system. We have already seen how words on nonattended channels can sometimes interrupt processing of attended channels. It is difficult to reconcile this result with an active model that requires active generation of matching speech responses in order to perceive phonemes. If it is difficult to see how a human could generate possibilities fast enough to make the active matching model work, it is even more difficult to imagine how he could actively match inputs on several channels simultaneously. But if matching is a prerequisite to understanding in the Halle and Stevens system, how can some meaningful components of speech get through to capture one's attention from a previously irrelevant channel? We are back to the paradox of attention.

SUGGESTED READINGS

There are a number of books which contain good summaries of the literature on pattern recognition relevant to psychology. Neisser (1967) provides the best review of the literature. His Chapter 3 gives an excellent description of the problems encountered by several theories of pattern recognition; his Chapters 4 and 7 are especially relevant to the perception of speech. An excellent review of the machine recognition of human language was serialized in three issues of the IEEE Spectrum by Lindgren (1965).

Most recent arguments, including all of the ones discussed here, are contained in the proceedings of a symposium held in Boston, Massachusetts in 1964 (Wathen-Dunn, 1967). In particular, see the papers by MacKay, Liberman *et al*, Stevens and Halle, Morton and Broadbent, Fant, and Sternberg. Reprints of a number of the earlier papers on pattern recognition have been collected by Uhr (1966). These books and review articles will readily lead the interested reader to the entire literature.

For the reader who wishes to learn more about the engineering side of pattern recognition, Arbib (1964) offers an easy introduction (see especially Chapter 2), and Nilsson (1965) provides a highly technical review (Chapters 1 and 2 are most relevant). The book by Minsky (1967) may also be of interest.

Papers on pattern recognition appear in engineering journals such as the *IEEE Transactions of Information Theory*, the *Journal of the Acoustical Society of America*, journals such as *Language and Speech,* and the standard psychology journals, such as *Psychological Review* and *Perception and Psychophysics.*

4

Visual Short-Term Memory

NEITHER attention nor pattern recognition operate in isolation. Both require that incoming sensory messages be interpreted with the aid of the context of the messages and their past history. Both context and history can be relevant only through the action of memory. To determine the immediate context of events, we need, at the least, a temporary storage system which keeps a memory of the recent past. To examine the entire past history of an event requires a permanent storage system.

Studies of attention, pattern perception, and memory are usually considered to be different and independent. Thus, although the three areas must eventually be combined into one picture of information processing, a review of present work in any one of these fields must proceed essentially independently of the others. We have already examined attention and pattern recognition. What can we say about memory?

MEMORY OF THE PRESENT

We start our study of memory with the most direct and immediate source, our introspections. There appear to be several types of memories which differ in their completeness, their duration, and the manner by which we get material in and out of them. We are continually aware of events which are just now happening, but this sense of the immediate present fades into a hazy recollection of the past. Is the distinction between our clear memory of the present and our vague memory of the

58

past real or is it an illusion? Again, the best clear statement of these different aspects of memory comes from William James.[1]

The stream of thought flows on; but most of its segments fall into the bottomless abyss of oblivion. Of some, no memory survives the instant of their passage. Of others, it is confined to a few moments, hours, or days. Others, again, leave vestiges which are indestructible, and by means of which they may be recalled as long as life endures. Can we explain these differences?

— — —

Well, the first manifestation of elementary habit is the slow dying away of an impressed movement on the neural matter, and its first effect in consciousness is this so-called elementary memory. But what elementary memory makes us aware of is the *just* past. The objects we feel in this directly intuited past differ from properly recollected objects. An object which is recollected, in the proper sense of that term, is one which has been absent from consciousness altogether, and now revives anew. It is brought back, recalled, fished up, so to speak, from a reservoir in which, with countless other objects, it lay buried and lost from view. But an object of primary memory is not thus brought back; it never was lost; its date was never cut off in consciousness from that of the immediately present moment. In fact it comes to us as belonging to the rearward portion of the present space of time, and not to the genuine past.

James distinguishes between our immediate knowledge of the past and what he calls "properly recollected objects." Our knowledge of the psychological present is too direct, immediate, and without conscious effort to be called a true memory, said James. True recollection from memory requires effort and the knowledge that what we are recovering differs from what we are presently experiencing. To distinguish these two phenomena, James proposes that the first, more immediate memory, be called *primary*, and the second, more indirect, *secondary*.

What relation does attention bear to recent memories? We have previously seen that the way in which we can divert our attention to events appears to require that all sensory events be analyzed in sufficient detail to determine their immediate relevance, a level of analysis that presumably involves memory. If this is so, our primary memory ought to contain a complete record of all events that have just occurred, not just those to which we are attending at the moment. James agreed, and found his proof in the following passage by Exner, a Viennese psychologist.[2]

[1] William James. *The Principles of Psychology*, Vol. 1. New York: Henry Holt and Co., 1890. Pages 643–647.
[2] James. *Op. cit.* Page 646. James is quoting from Exner in L. Hermann, *Handbuch der Physiologie*, Vol. 2. Page 282 (1880).

Exner writes:

Impressions to which we are inattentive leave so brief an image in the memory that it is usually overlooked. When deeply absorbed, we do not hear the clock strike. But our attention may awake after the striking has ceased, and we may then count off the strokes. Such examples are often found in daily life. We can also prove the existence of this *primary memory-image*, as it may be called, in another person, even when his attention is completely absorbed elsewhere. Ask someone, e.g., to count the lines of a printed page as fast as he can, and whilst this is going on walk a few steps about the room. Then, when the person has done counting, ask him where you stood. He will always reply quite definitely that you have walked. Analogous experiments may be done with vision. This primary memory-image is, whether attention have been turned to the impression or not, an extremely lively one, but is subjectively quite distinct from every sort of after-image or hallucination. . . . It vanishes, if not caught by attention, in the course of a few seconds. Even when the original impression is attended to, the liveliness of its image in memory fades fast.

This tantalizing reference to the rapid fading from primary memory of unattended events remains almost our only connection between the work on attention and the work on memory. Not much can be added to Exner's observations for little quantitative work has been done on this problem since 1880.

Let us continue the study of immediate memories; how much do we retain of events which have just previously occurred? Our intuition suggests we keep a very accurate record. When I shut my eyes for an instant, I can still picture the disarray on my desk with what appears to be perfect accuracy. This picture is not a retinal after-image either, for I can actively attend to my view of the sea, the surf, and the snow-covered mountains without impeding my recollection of the desk. But is the impression of complete recollection of just-experienced events accurate?

When we try to determine exactly how much is retained of an immediate memory, we can measure only a very small quantity. If a person is asked to name what he has just seen, he stumbles, able to recall but a handful of items. In fact, the results of a large number of carefully controlled experiments indicate that humans can usually recall only a very limited number of items which have just been presented to them—from as few as four to, perhaps, ten items. The rather low limit on the number of new (and unrelated) items we can recall after a single exposure is one of the puzzles of memory. Meaningful material is relatively easy to learn, but we have trouble with isolated items. The contents of our immediate recall of unrelated material is commonly called the memory span, but this is a misleading phrase; it should be called the memory limitation. Why is there this apparent contradiction between the richness of our impressions of recent events and the sparseness of our recall of those impressions?

One reason for the apparent discrepancy is that the very act of recalling one event may cause us to forget others. It was not until 100 years after Exner that this notion was tested, and even then, the experiments only began to answer the puzzle. Let us look at one such study, performed in the late 1950's at Harvard University by George Sperling.

THE INFORMATION IN BRIEF PRESENTATIONS *

GEORGE SPERLING

How much can be seen in a single brief exposure? This is an important problem because our normal mode of seeing greatly resembles a sequence of brief exposures. Erdmann and Dodge (1898) showed that in reading, for example, the eye assimilates information only in the brief pauses between its quick saccadic movements. The problem of what can be seen in one brief exposure, however, remains unsolved. The difficulty is that the simple expedient of instructing the observer of a single brief exposure to report what he has just seen is inadequate. When complex stimuli consisting of a number of letters are tachistoscopically presented, observers enigmatically insist that they have seen more than they can remember afterwards, that is, report afterwards. The apparently simple question: "What did you see?" requires the observer to report both what he remembers and what he has forgotten.

The statement that *more is seen than can be remembered* implies two things. First, it implies a memory limit, that is, a limit on the (memory) report. Such a limit on the number of items which can be given in the report following any brief stimulation has, in fact, been generally observed; it is called the span of attention, apprehension, or immediate-memory (cf. Miller, 1956a). Second, *to see more than is remembered* implies that more information is available during, and perhaps for a short time after, the stimulus than can be reported. The considerations about available information are quite similar, whether the information is available for an hour (as it is in a book that is borrowed for an hour), or whether the information is available for only a fraction of a second (as in a stimulus which is exposed for only a fraction of a second). In either case it is quite probable that for a limited period of time more informa-

* George Sperling. The information available in brief visual presentations, *Psychological Monographs*. 1960, 74, whole number 498. Pages 1–2. Copyright 1960 by the American Psychological Association and reproduced by permission.

tion will be available than can be reported. It is also true that initially, in both examples, the information is available to vision.

In order to circumvent the memory limitation in determining the information that becomes available following a brief exposure, it is obvious that the observer must not be required to give a report which exceeds his memory span. If the number of letters in the stimulus exceeds his memory span, then he cannot give a whole report of all the letters. Therefore, the observer must be required to give only a partial report of the stimulus contents. Partial reporting of available information is, of course, just what is required by ordinary schoolroom examinations and by other methods of sampling available information.

An examiner can determine, even in a short test, approximately how much the student knows. The length of the test is not so important as that the student not be told the test questions too far in advance. Similarly, an observer may be "tested" on what he has seen in a brief exposure of a complex visual stimulus. Such a test requires only a partial report. The specific instruction which indicates which part of the stimulus is to be reported is then given only after termination of the stimulus. On each trial the instruction, which calls for a specified part of the stimulus, is randomly chosen from a set of possible instructions which cover the whole stimulus. By repeating the interrogation (sampling) procedure many times, many different random samples can be obtained of an observer's performance on each of the various parts of the stimulus. The data obtained thereby make feasible the estimate of the total information that was available to the observer from which to draw his report on the average trial.

The time at which the instruction is given determines the time at which available information is sampled. By suitable coding, the instruction may be given at any time: before, during, or after the stimulus presentation. Not only the available information immediately following the termination of the stimulus, but a continuous function relating the amount of information available to the time of instruction may be obtained by such a procedure.

In his experiments, Sperling presented visual arrays of English letters briefly to his subjects and then asked for only partial reporting of the image. Basically, he presented a set of 12 letters, arranged in 3 rows of 4 letters. Then, after a brief exposure, Sperling signaled which letters were to be recalled by presenting an acoustical tone of high, medium, or low frequency. A high tone, for example, meant that the top row should be reported. By controlling both the component of the image which was to be reported and the delay between presentation of the letters and the tone, Sperling was able to minimize the detrimental effect of early reports on later ones, while getting a systematic measure of the rate of decay of the sensory image. The sampling procedure insured that subjects were tested over all parts of the sensory image, so it was possible to infer the total capacity of the sensory memory from the repeated partial reports. Not surprisingly, Sperling found that the sensory image does in fact contain much more information than had previously been reported.

Sperling argued that the contradiction between what we see and what we recall is based simply on the problems of testing human subjects. The act of recall causes forgetting. Actually then, Sperling is proposing a more complex system than we envisaged before. He suggested that there are at least *three* stages of memory. The first is a complete sensory image of just-occurring events, the second, an immediate or short-term memory which contains the limited information we are able to extract from the rapidly decaying, sensory image, and the third (implied, but not mentioned), a permanent or long-term memory with a very large capacity.

With three different memory systems, we now face additional problems. When we postulate different memory systems we have an obligation to explain how they might be related and how they differ. This task is much more difficult than the task of studying the properties of any one system. It is possible to construct many models of the interrelationship among various memory systems; the limit is given only by the limits of imagination. It is much more difficult to test the implications of each model and restrict the set of possibilities. Let us examine how Sperling goes about this process. The models that follow come from a paper that was written in 1966, six years after the original research was reported. They should be viewed as an example of how experimentation and theorizing is performed, not as a final authoritative description of the memory process. The research will still continue so that future years should bring further refinements.

THREE MODELS FOR SHORT-TERM MEMORY *

GEORGE SPERLING

Model 1

When a row of letters is exposed briefly, i.e., for 1/20th sec, an adult subject con reproduce about 4 or 5 of the letters. The simplest model for the action

* George Sperling. Successive approximations to a model for short-term memory. Sanders, A. F. (Ed.), in *Attention and Performance*. Amsterdam: North-Holland Publishing Co., 1967. (A special edition of *Acta Psychologia*, 27.) Pages 286–288, 290–292. Copyright 1967 by North-Holland Publishing Co., Amsterdam. With permission of the author and the North-Holland Publishing Co.

of reproducing visually presented letters might be organized into two main components: (1) a visual memory containing the letters (called visual information storage) and (2) a translation component, which can translate a visual image of the letters into a series of motor actions; namely, copying the letters onto a piece of paper (Fig. 1). The limited memory span of the subject might be represented in the model by progressive deterioration—a fading into illegibility—of the contents of visual storage. While the subject is writing, the contents of his visual memory are decaying, so that when he finally comes to write the fifth or sixth letter his visual memory of the stimulus no longer is legible.

Without elaborating further on the difficulties of Model 1, we can reject it immediately for one basic reason: before the subject begins to write the letters, his visual image of the letters has already disappeared . . . Having shown that letters are not stored visually until they are reproduced, we must now determine the form in which they are stored.

Model 2

Occasionally a subject, when he is writing down letters, can be heard to mumble the letters as he is writing them. His tendency to say the letters aloud can be emphasized by playing loud noise into his ears. Noise itself does not seem to alter performance in any other significant way. We have used this technique, together with a microphone placed near the subject's mouth, to record the actual letters the subject is saying. We also recorded automatically whenever the subject was writing. The most interesting results with this technique are obtained when the subject is required to wait (e.g., for 20 sec) after the stimulus exposure before writing the letters. He repeats (rehearses) the entire letter sequence several times with a pause between each repetition during the interval. Then, at the time of writing each letter, he also may speak it simultaneously.

Rehearsal suggests an obvious memory mechanism. The subject says a let-

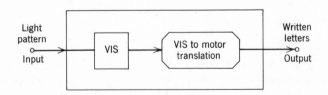

Fig. 1. Model 1. The large box represents the subject. Arrows indicate the direction of information flow. The components are visual information storage (VIS) and a translator. The translator converts an input (the memory of a letter) into an output (a series of motor actions) which result in a written representation of the letter.

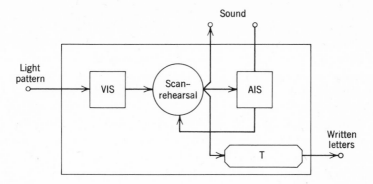

Fig. 2. Model 2. VIS = visual information storage, AIS = auditory information storage, T = translator.

ter, hears himself saying it, and then remembers the auditory image. As the auditory image fades, he repeats it to refresh it. Most of our subjects do not vocalize during recall, but they all concur in stating that they rehearse subvocally. Therefore, we assume that the sound-image of a letter can enter auditory memory directly from subvocal rehearsal without the necessity of actually being converted into sound and passing into the external world. These relations are illustrated in Fig. 2.

The auditory nature of subvocal rehearsal can be emphasized by playing distracting speech into one's ears during rehearsal. The speech seems to emanate from one set of locations in space (the ears) while one's rehearsal is heard as an internal voice speaking from the center of the head. External sound also can be used as a clock against which to measure the rate of subvocal rehearsal. Another method of measuring the rate of subvocal rehearsal is to ask subjects to rehearse a sequence of letters subvocally 10 times and to signal when through. This may be compared to a vocal rehearsal of the same sequence. All these indirect measures of the rate of subvocal rehearsal indicate that, while it may be slightly faster than vocal rehearsal, it is basically the same process (cf. Landauer, 1962). The maximum possible rate is about 6 letters per second but, in memory experiments, maximum rates of about 3 letters per second are more typical.

The existence of auditory memory in visual reproduction tasks also may be inferred from the deterioration in performance which occurs when the stimulus letters sound alike (B, C, D, etc.). We have studied a large variety of tasks in which stimuli were presented visually or auditorily and found almost the same rule to apply to both modalities of presentation. When the memory load is small (about 2.5 letters in an auditory task, 3 letters in a visual task) it makes little difference to performance whether the stimulus letters sound alike or sound different. Additional letters beyond the minimal number are remembered only about half as well when they sound alike as when they sound different. This dependence of performance on the sound of letters—even in a task which nominally involves only looking and writing—is of practical as well as of theoretical importance (Conrad, 1963; Sperling, 1963).

According to Model 2, stimulus letters first are retained in visual storage. They are rehearsed, one at a time (i.e., converted from a visual to an auditory form), and then remembered in auditory storage. Subsequently they may be rehearsed again and again as required until they are written down. The limits on performance may arise either from the limited duration visual storage (so that some letters decay before they can be rehearsed) or from the limited capacity of the rehearsal-auditory storage loop, depending on the stimulating conditions.

Attractive as Model 2 seems, it is inadequate for the following reason: it is possible to generate an image in visual storage which has a duration of definitely less than .1 sec and from which 3 letters can be reported. This would require a rehearsal rate of over 30 letters per second, which clearly is completely beyond the capabilities of the rehearsal processes described for Model 2.

— — —

Model 3

In Model 3 (Fig. 3), the scan-rehearsal component of Model 2 is subdivided into three separate components. The first of these is a scan component which determines—within a limited range—the sequence of locations from which information is entered into subsequent components. The extent to which the subject can vary his order of scanning is a current research problem. In very brief exposures, the variation in scanning may be limited to changing the rate of

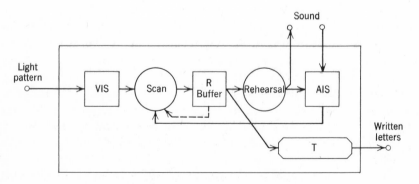

Fig. 3. *Model 3.* (See Fig. 2) R-buffer = recognition buffer-memory.

acquisition at different locations—information processing beginning simultaneously at all locations. On the other hand, the overall rate of information flow through the scanner must be limited.

The second new component is the recognition buffer-memory. It converts the visual image of a letter provided by the scanner into a 'program of motor-instructions,' and stores these instructions. This program of motor instructions, when it is executed by the rehearsal component, constitutes rehearsal. The important idea embodied in the recognition buffer-memory is that the program of motor-instructions for a rehearsal can be set up in a very short time (e.g., 50 msec for 3 letters) compared to the time necessary to execute it (e.g., 500 msec for 3 letters).

The recognition buffer is efficient partly because the programs for rehearsing several letters can be set up in it simultaneously. However, the major gain in speed derives from the assumption that setting up a program to rehearse a letter is inherently a faster process than executing the program, i.e., rehearsing the letter. In fact, the biological organization of motor systems is extremely hierarchical. Thus the program in the recognition-buffer could be a program to call a program, etc., and the ultimate representation at the top of such a pyramid could be called quickly.

The rehearsal component executes the rehearsal, which then is entered and remembered temporarily in auditory storage. The memory of the rehearsal in auditory storage is scanned, the auditory image is converted to motor-instruction in the recognition-buffer, and a second rehearsal is executed. This loop continues until the response is called for and the letters are written down. I know almost nothing about the translation of the memory of a letter to its written representation except that it occurs, and therefore must be represented in the model. It has been represented in parallel with rehearsal because writing a letter so often is accompanied by vocalization.

CONSCIOUSNESS IN THE MEMORY MODELS

One can know the contents of the consciousness of another individual only insofar as they are expressed by his behavior, particularly by his verbal behavior. In the models, this structure would induce us to look for evidence of consciousness at the level of the rehearsal unit. However, one also must admit that a person who is unable to speak or act may still retain consciousness. The critical aspect of the contents of consciousness is that they normally are capable of being verbalized or acted upon. Within the limits of the tasks for which Model 3 was proposed, we can identify the contents of the scan component with the contents of consciousness. This is because the scan component contains the information upon which actions are performed.

There are several inferences to be drawn from this identification. When contents of visual memory are not scanned before they fade away, they never become conscious. And, we are unconscious of all contents of our auditory memory except those being scanned. Another inference is that if the contents of a memory cannot be scanned, they are not accessible to consciousness. The untransformed contents of the recognition buffer-memory are not accessible to scanning and therefore never the objects of consciousness. This makes it indeed a mysterious component; it cannot be observed directly either from within or from without! However, this inaccessibility should not surprise us. It is axiomatic that in any system which examines itself there ultimately must be some part of the mechanism which is inaccessible to examination from within. The recognition buffer-memory is such a part in the human memory mechanism.

Aside from the formal structure of the models, Sperling introduces several important concepts in his analyses of the memory process. One is the notion of rehearsal, a type of inner speech by which humans are able to maintain a limited amount of material in memory indefinitely. We all use rehearsal when we remember something, for example, a telephone number, by "saying it to ourselves." Rehearsal also helps us to learn material, presumably by helping to transfer material from temporary to more permanent systems.

Rehearsal is a vocal process in that we act as if we were saying something to ourselves. This does not necessarily imply that we are actually speaking or even using any of our speech mechanisms. The primary implications of rehearsal lie in its more obvious characteristics. First, it is based on the spoken word. Material that is learned or retained through rehearsal appears to be stored in a form that is related to the way it is spoken. Thus, mistakes in retention are likely to bear acoustical relations to the correct item, even if the material was originally presented visually. Second, rehearsal is a serial process; only one item can be rehearsed at any one time. Third, it is slow; Sperling estimates it to take place at the rate of 3 to 6 items per second.

Very little is known about rehearsal, except that it appears to be beneficial—perhaps even necessary—to the learning of verbal material. There are many opinions on the matter and almost no facts. Some psychologists equate rehearsal with a deliberate attempt to repeat verbal material to oneself. Other psychologists believe that rehearsal need not necessarily be a conscious process; it may really not be related to speech at all. Some believe that rehearsal aids retention in exactly the same way that repeated presentations of an item help in its retention. Others believe that rehearsal represents a more fundamental operation than presentation: the two need not be similar. For all of these beliefs and opinions, no one is able to suggest satisfactory reasons for *why* or *how* rehearsal is so important to the memory process. Moreover, because rehearsal is not easily susceptible to measurement, few people have any ideas about how to start studying the issues. Everyone, however, seems to agree about its importance.

It is an easy matter to teach subjects how to rehearse or to give them distracting tasks to do so they cannot rehearse. (A favorite task which seems to prevent subjects from rehearsing previously presented material is to have them count backwards by threes, aloud, and at a rapid rate.) These manipulations change the amount and character of material that can be remembered. Thus, although no one really understands the nature or purpose of rehearsal, it is easy to control the way that subjects do it, thereby controlling the way that material is learned. We shall return to the discussion of rehearsal several more times throughout the course of the book. Let us conclude this discussion simply by noting the similarity of conditions that are known to disrupt rehearsal and conditions which disrupt the amount of attention that can be given to a task. In fact, rehearsal of material is sometimes equated to the attention one pays to the material. Anything which interferes with that attention also interferes with rehearsal. The same variables, types of tasks, and theories which one applies to attention appear to be relevant to rehearsal as well.

Another feature of Sperling's models is the introduction of other types of memory systems. In his third model, Sperling would have information which has been extracted ("scanned") from the visual information storage end up in an auditory storage. Although the point is not discussed, auditory storage is still a temporary mechanism, probably corresponding to the primary store of James.

The processes proposed in these models apply only to the retention of verbal material. The retention of nonverbal sounds, visual scenes, and physical activity cannot be treated by this scheme. There is some evidence that we do rehearse body action, complete with very slight movements. (Imagine yourself doing some familiar task or sport. Notice how the appropriate muscles tense up at the relevant times. Some athletes believe that they can improve their performance by this type of motor rehearsal.) Obviously, we need not verbalize visual scenes in order that they be remembered. Just how complex images are retained and what the role of verbalization and rehearsal is in the retention of grammatical material are unexplored problem areas in the study of memory.

Do not think that Sperling's models or experiments represent the consensus of opinion about sensory and short-term memory. In the interest of the clarity and continuity of this chapter, a good deal of dissenting opinion has been ignored. There are psychologists who disagree with the experimental evidence Sperling has presented. There are some who admit the evidence, but disagree with the interpretations. There are also a good number of psychologists who feel that there is little value in making distinctions among different memory processes, for they believe that memory is one single phenomenon which simply appears to be different when examined by different experimental techniques.

An ever-increasing amount of evidence does seem to favor the interpretation of human memory as a part of a complex chain of processes, similar to those proposed by Sperling, which are involved in the handling of information from its sensory representation to its permanent storage. These processes appear to have different functional modes of excitation, although the issue of whether different physical structures are involved is not yet settled. These modes represent the distinction between the various memory systems we have discussed here: a sensory memory, a primary (or short-term) memory, and a secondary (or permanent) memory.

To continue our analysis of the memory process, we now turn to the next stage in the process: primary memory.

SUGGESTED READINGS

This chapter is skimpy in content in order to emphasize the character of the proposed models. The work on visual short-term memory has also led to research on visual backward masking. Basically, this came about through a set of experiments very similar to those of Sperling. Sperling used an auditory tone in his first experiments and was only able to cue his subjects to recall a specific row of letters. Averbach and Coriell got subjects to recall single letters by cueing them with a visual pointer, presented at varying delays after the finish of the letter display. When the marker was a circle, surrounding the letter to be recalled, an interesting effect was discovered: the subjects reported seeing an empty circle, as if the presentation of the circle had erased the image of the letter. Averbach, Coriell, and Sperling have used this erasure technique to estimate the time decay of the image in visual short-term memory. Meanwhile, a number of investigators have worried about how this "backward masking" comes about. Some of the ensuing discussions have raised doubts on the type of memory process proposed by Averbach, Coriell, and Sperling. If you wish to pursue this line of investigation, see Averbach and Coriell (1961), Averbach and Sperling

(1961), and the review by Kahneman (1968). A summary of the arguments (and references to the other point of view) can be found in Neisser (1967, Chapter 2).

An 18-minute movie, featuring Averbach and Coriell, is available from the Bell Telephone Company. The movie, entitled "Short-Term Visual Memory," illustrates the experimental procedure, the phenomenon of erasure, and the theoretical interpretations placed on the results.

Most research on this problem is discussed in the following journals:

Journal of Experimental Psychology
Perception and Psychophysics
Perceptual and Motor Skills
Psychological Review
Psychonomic Science

5

Primary Memory

In the early 1950's, the mathematical theory of information played an important role in the thoughts, theories, and experiments of psychologists. The reasons are fairly obvious. Communication engineers had developed a formal structure for discussing the effects of channel capacity, noise, and transmission rate on the amount of information that any message could contain. Psychologists realized that the human could be viewed as an information processing device, reducing and transmitting the information contained in the environment through the sensory system and into some encoding in memory. Thus stated, the psychologists and engineers were studying similar problems. Limitations on memory capacity could be interpreted as limitations on our ability to receive information.

The information concept ran into one serious problem in studies of memory: it didn't work. This is not to say that the basic concepts of information theory were not valuable, for they did provide useful new interpretations of psychological phenomena. The problem was that the way the communication engineer measured information just did not seem to apply to the human.

THE MAGICAL NUMBER PROBLEM

In 1956, George Miller summarized a good deal of the research on human information processing in a paper that has since become widely known as "the 7 ± 2" paper. In this paper, Miller discussed the application of the concept of channel capacity to studies of memory and absolute judgments. His discussion of the memory problem is directly relevant to our discussion here, so we start with a brief look at Miller's explanation of information theory followed by his discussion of memory.

THE MAGICAL NUMBER SEVEN, PLUS
OR MINUS TWO *

GEORGE A. MILLER

My problem is that I have been persecuted by an integer. For seven years this number has followed me around, has intruded in my most private data, and has assaulted me from the pages of our most public journals. This number assumes a variety of disguises, being sometimes a little larger and sometimes a little smaller than usual, but never changing so much as to be unrecognizable. The persistence with which this number plagues me is far more than a random accident. There is, to quote a famous senator, a design behind it, some pattern governing its appearances. Either there really is something unusual about the number or else I am suffering from delusions of persecution.

I shall begin my case history by telling you about some experiments that tested how accurately people can assign numbers to the magnitudes of various aspects of a stimulus. In the traditional language of psychology these would be called experiments in absolute judgment. Historical accident, however, has decreed that they should have another name. We now call them experiments on the capacity of people to transmit information. Since these experiments would not have been done without the appearance of information theory on the psychological scene, and since the results are analyzed in terms of the concepts of information theory, I shall have to preface my discussion with a few remarks about this theory.

INFORMATION MEASUREMENT

The "amount of information" is exactly the same concept that we have talked about for years under the name of "variance."[1] The equations are dif-

[1] "Variance" here refers to the statistical concept of the amount of dispersion or variability there is in a set of measurements. Those of you unfamiliar with the concept will find it satisfactory to substitute the word "variability" every place that

* George A. Miller. The magical number seven, plus or minus two: some limits on our capacity for processing information. *Psychol. Rev.*, 1956, **63**, 81–97. Copyright 1956 by the American Psychological Association. With permission of the author and publisher.

ferent, but if we hold tight to the idea that anything that increases the variance also increases the amount of information we cannot go far astray.

The advantages of this new way of talking about variance are simple enough. Variance is always stated in terms of the unit of measurement—inches, pounds, volts, etc.—whereas the amount of information is a dimensionless quantity. Since the information in a discrete statistical distribution does not depend upon the unit of measurement, we can extend the concept to situations where we have no metric and we would not ordinarily think of using the variance. And it also enables us to compare results obtained in quite different experimental situations where it would be meaningless to compare variances based on different metrics. So there are some good reasons for adopting the newer concept.

The similarity of variance and amount of information might be explained this way: When we have a large variance, we are very ignorant about what is going to happen. If we are very ignorant, then when we make the observation it gives us a lot of information. On the other hand, if the variance is very small, we know in advance how our observation must come out, so we get little information from making the observation.

— — —

If the human observer is a reasonable kind of communication system, then when we increase the amount of input information the transmitted information will increase at first and will eventually level off at some asymptotic value. This asymptotic value we take to be the *channel capacity* of the observer: it represents the greatest amount of information that he can give us about the stimulus on the basis of an absolute judgment. The channel capacity is the upper limit on the extent to which the observer can match his responses to the stimuli we give him.

Now just a brief word about the *bit* and we can begin to look at some data. One bit of information is the amount of information that we need to make a decision between two equally likely alternatives. If we must decide whether a man is less than six feet tall or more than six feet tall and if we know that the chances are 50-50, then we need one bit of information. Notice that this unit of information does not refer in any way to the unit of length that we use—feet, inches, centimeters, etc. However you measure the man's height, we still need just one bit of information.

Miller uses "variance." To state Miller's point in terms of variability: if everybody in the world had exactly the same height, then a new measurement of that height would convey no new information. If heights vary, however, the measurements are meaningful and convey information. In fact, the more unexpected the result (the greater the variability), the more information contained in the measurement. Variability (and variance) is always stated in the units of the thing being measured. Thus, we might say that the variability of heights is plus or minus so many inches.

Two bits of information enable us to decide among four equally likely alternatives. Three bits of information enable us to decide among eight equally likely alternatives. Four bits of information decide among 16 alternatives, five among 32, and so on. That is to say, if there are 32 equally likely alternatives, we must make five successive binary decisions, worth one bit each, before we know which alternative is correct. So the general rule is simple: every time the number of alternatives is increased by a factor of two, one bit of information is added.

There are two ways we might increase the amount of input information. We could increase the rate at which we give information to the observer, so that the amount of information per unit time would increase. Or we could ignore the time variable completely and increase the amount of input information by increasing the number of alternative stimuli. In the absolute judgment experiment we are interested in the second alternative. We give the observer as much time as he wants to make his response; we simply increase the number of alternative stimuli among which he must discriminate and look to see where confusions begin to occur. Confusions will appear near the point that we are calling his "channel capacity."

Miller summarized a number of studies on absolute judgments and memory and found "a clear and definite limit to the limit with which we can identify absolutely the magnitude of a unidimensional stimulus variable." The limit is called the span of absolute judgment and it usually lies somewhere in the neighborhood of seven. Increased accuracy of judgments over that can be obtained by a number of techniques. "The three most important of these devices are (a) to make relative rather than absolute judgments; or, if that is not possible, (b) to increase the number of dimensions along which the stimuli can differ; or (c) to arrange the task in such a way that we make a sequence of several absolute judgments in a row."

The span of immediate memory behaves differently than does our ability to make absolute judgments. Immediate memory appears to be limited by the number of items, regardless of the information content of the items. Because of this, Miller found that the apparent memory span could be increased by a recoding process. Normally, when we try to remember a list of items, we can immediately recall about seven of them. If, however, we were first to learn a code word for every possible pair of items we could easily retain a string of seven code words. Thus, without overloading our normal memory span of seven, we could fool an observer into thinking that our span was actually 14 items. This process of increasing the memory span by efficient grouping of old items into new items, Miller called *chunking*. Miller concludes: [2]

[2] George Miller, The magical number seven. *Op. cit.* Pages 93–96.

RECODING

In order to speak more precisely, therefore, we must recognize the importance of grouping or organizing the input sequence into units or chunks. Since the memory span is a fixed number of chunks, we can increase the number of bits of information that it contains simply by building larger and larger chunks each chunk containing more information than before.

A man just beginning to learn radio-telegraphic code hears each *dit* and *dah* as a separate chunk. Soon he is able to organize these sounds into letters and then he can deal with the letters as chunks. Then the letters organize themselves as words, which are still larger chunks, and he begins to hear whole phrases. I do not mean that each step is a discrete process, or that plateaus must appear in his learning curve, for surely the levels of organization are achieved at different rates and overlap each other during the learning process. I am simply pointing to the obvious fact that the dits and dahs are organized by learning into patterns and that as these larger chunks emerge the amount of message that the operator can remember increases correspondingly. In the terms I am proposing to use, the operator learns to increase the bits per chunk.

In the jargon of communication theory, this process would be called *recoding*. The input is given in a code that contains many chunks with few bits per chunk. The operator recodes the input into another code that contains fewer chunks with more bits per chunk. There are many ways to do this recoding, but probably the simplest is to group the input events, apply a new name to the group, and then remember the new name rather than the original input events.

Since I am convinced that this process is a very general and important one for psychology, I want to tell you about a demonstration experiment that should make perfectly explicit what I am talking about. This experiment was conducted by Sidney Smith and was reported by him before the Eastern Psychological Association in 1954.

Begin with the observed fact that people can repeat back eight decimal digits, but only nine binary digits. Since there is a large discrepancy in the amount of information recalled in these two cases, we suspect at once that a recoding procedure could be used to increase the span of immediate memory for binary digits. In Table 1 a method for grouping and renaming is illustrated. Along the top is a sequence of 18 binary digits, far more than any subject was able to recall after a single presentation. In the next line these same binary digits are grouped by pairs. Four possible pairs can occur: 00 is renamed 0, 01 is renamed 1, 10 is renamed 2, and 11 is renamed 3. That is

Table 1   Ways of Recoding Sequences of Binary Digits

Binary Digits (Bits)	1	0	1	0	0	0	1	0	0	1	1	1	0	0	1	1	1	0
2:1 Chunks	10		10		00		10		01		11		00		11		10	
Recoding	2		2		0		2		1		3		0		3		2	
3:1 Chunks	101			000			100			111			001			110		
Recoding	5			0			4			7			1			6		
4:1 Chunks	1010				0010				0111				0011				10	
Recoding	10				2				7				3					
5:1 Chunks	10100					01001					11001					110		
Recoding	20					9					25							

to say, we recode from a base-two arithmetic to a base-four arithmetic. In the recoded sequence there are now just nine digits to remember, and this is almost within the span of immediate memory. In the next line the same sequence of binary digits is regrouped into chunks of three. There are eight possible sequences of three, so we give each sequence a new name between 0 and 7. Now we have recoded from a sequence of 18 binary digits into a sequence of 6 octal digits, and this is well within the span of immediate memory. In the last two lines the binary digits are grouped by fours and by fives and are given decimal-digit names from 0 to 15 and from 0 to 31.

It is reasonably obvious that this kind of recoding increases the bits per chunk, and packages the binary sequence into a form that can be retained within the span of immediate memory. So Smith assembled 20 subjects and measured their spans for binary and octal digits. The spans were 9 for binaries and 7 for octals. Then he gave each recoding scheme to five of the subjects. They studied the recoding until they said they understood it—for about 5 or 10 minutes. Then he tested their span for binary digits again while they tried to use the recoding schemes they had studied.

The recoding schemes increased their span for binary digits in every case. But the increase was not as large as we had expected on the basis of their span for octal digits. Since the discrepancy increased as the recoding ratio increased, we reasoned that the few minutes the subjects had spent learning the recoding schemes had not been sufficient. Apparently the translation from one code to the other must be almost automatic or the subject will lose part of the next group while he is trying to remember the translation of the last group.

Since the 4:1 and 5:1 ratios require considerable study, Smith decided

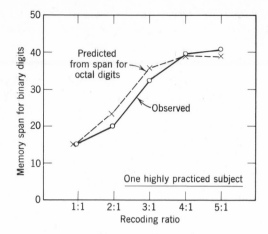

Fig. 1. The span of immediate memory for binary digits is plotted as a function of the recoding procedure used. The predicted function is obtained by multiplying the span for octals by 2, 3 and 3.3 for recoding into base 4, base 8, and base 10, respectively.

to imitate Ebbinghaus and do the experiment on himself. With Germanic patience he drilled himself on each recoding successively, and obtained the results shown in Fig. 1. Here the data follow along rather nicely with the results you would predict on the basis of his span for octal digits. He could remember 12 octal digits. With the 2:1 recoding, these 12 chunks were worth 24 binary digits. With the 3:1 recoding they were worth 36 binary digits. With the 4:1 and 5:1 recodings, they were worth about 40 binary digits.

It is a little dramatic to watch a person get 40 binary digits in a row and then repeat them back without error. However, if you think of this merely as a mnemonic trick for extending the memory span, you will miss the more important point that is implicit in nearly all such mnemonic devices. The point is that recoding is an extremely powerful weapon for increasing the amount of information that we can deal with. In one form or another we use recoding constantly in our daily behavior.

In my opinion the most customary kind of recoding that we do all the time is to translate into a verbal code. When there is a story or an argument or an idea that we want to remember, we usually try to rephrase it "in our own words." When we witness some event we want to remember, we make a verbal description of the event and then remember our verbalization. Upon recall we recreate by secondary elaboration the details that seem consistent with the particular verbal recoding we happen to have made. The well-known experiment by Carmichael, Hogan, and Walter (1932) on the influence that names have on the recall of visual figures is one demonstration of the process.

The inaccuracy of the testimony of eyewitnesses is well known in legal psychology, but the distortions of testimony are not random—they follow naturally from the particular recoding that the witness used, and the particular recoding he used depends upon his whole life history. Our language is tremendously useful for repackaging material into a few chunks rich in information. I suspect that imagery is a form of recoding, too, but images seem much harder to get at operationally and to study experimentally than the more symbolic kinds of recoding.

It seems probable that even memorization can be studied in these terms. The process of memorizing may be simply the formation of chunks, or groups of items that go together, until there are few enough chunks so that we can recall all the items. The work by Bousfield and Cohen (1955) on the occurrence of clustering in the recall of words is especially interesting in this respect.

SUMMARY

I have come to the end of the data that I wanted to present, so I would like now to make some summarizing remarks.

First, the span of absolute judgment and the span of immediate memory impose severe limitations on the amount of information that we are able to receive, process, and remember. By organizing the stimulus input simultaneously into several dimensions and successively into a sequence of chunks, we manage to break (or at least stretch) this informational bottleneck.

Second, the process of recoding is a very important one in human psychology and deserves much more explicit attention than it has received. In particular, the kind of linguistic recoding that people do seems to me to be the very lifeblood of the thought processes. Recoding procedures are a constant concern to clinicians, social psychologists, linguists, and anthropologists and yet, probably because recoding is less accessible to experimental manipulation than nonsense syllables or T mazes, the traditional experimental psychologist has contributed little or nothing to their analysis. Nevertheless, experimental techniques can be used, methods of recoding can be specified, behavioral indicants can be found. And I anticipate that we will find a very orderly set of relations describing what now seems an uncharted wilderness of individual differences.

Third, the concepts and measures provided by the theory of information provide a quantitative way of getting at some of these questions. The theory provides us with a yardstick for calibrating our stimulus materials and for measuring the performance of our subjects. In the interests of communication I have suppressed the technical details of information measurement and have tried to express the ideas in more familiar terms; I hope this paraphrase will not lead you to think they are not useful in research. Informational concepts have already proved valuable in the study of discrimination and of language; they promise a great deal in the study of learning and memory; and it has even been proposed that they can be useful in the study of concept formation. A lot of questions that seemed fruitless twenty or thirty years ago may now be worth another look. In fact, I feel that my story here must stop just as it begins to get really interesting.

And finally, what about the magical number seven? What about the seven wonders of the world, the seven seas, the seven deadly sins, the seven daughters of Atlas in the Pleiades, the seven ages of man, the seven levels of hell, the seven primary colors, the seven notes of the musical scale, and the seven days of the week? What about the seven-point rating scale, the seven categories for absolute judgment, the seven objects in the span of attention, and the seven digits in the span of immediate memory? For the present I propose to withhold judgment. Perhaps there is something deep and profound behind all these sevens, something just calling out for us to discover it. But I suspect that it is only a pernicious, Pythagorean coincidence.

The differences between our ability to make absolute judgments and to retain things in immediate memory result from differences in the types of information processing involved. When we try to make an absolute judgment we are trying to encode information. That is, we are trying to categorize the stimulus input according to previously learned classifications. The span of immediate memory, however, is a measure of our ability to retain material which has already been encoded; this is a very important distinction. The limit on span seems to be determined by the number of items we are trying to retain; the limit on absolute judgments seems to be determined by the number of judgments we are trying to make.

By the time something gets into immediate memory it has already received a good deal of processing. For one thing, it seems to have been translated into meaningful units. It makes sense that the number of meaningful components which we can retain is not related to the amount of information contained in the original stimulus material. It also makes sense that we can improve our apparent memory span by recoding or "chunking" the items we are trying to remember. After all, any meaningful item ought to be just as difficult to remember as any other meaningful item regardless of the number of physical attributes actually represented. In fact, it would be surprising if the limit of immediate memory were related to stimulus parameters. Meanings attached to words have little relationship to the sound or shape of what we speak or write (with the special exception of onomatopoeic words), so why should our memory for these meanings have any relationship to simple stimulus parameters?

The immediate memory which we are discussing here is quite different from the visual information storage of Chapter 4. The visual storage maintained an image of the stimulus for a duration sufficient to let the encoding of visual shapes into meaningful components take place. In the models of Chapter 4, the output of visual short-term memory entered an auditory information storage. That auditory storage is the immediate memory of this chapter.

The important question we must ask about immediate memory concerns the limit on its span. Why seven items? Why a limit at all? This limited memory is very strange because there does not seem to be any limit on the amount of material that we are able to learn: we can retain millions, even billions of things. How do we learn those millions of items if we have such a small capacity in immediate memory? These issues define the area of study now called "short-term memory." The questions and the area are not new; later we shall read what William James said about it in 1890, but modern concepts of the properties of short-term memory developed about the time that Miller wrote his article on the magical number seven. The name "short-term memory" really serves to define a type of experiment rather than a process that takes place in humans. Therefore, before we turn to theories of immediate or short-term memory (later, we shall call it "primary memory"), let us detour slightly in order to review the experimental procedures that are now in common use.

EXPERIMENTS ON SHORT-TERM MEMORY

EXPERIMENTAL PROCEDURES

There are many ways to test a subject's recollection of previously presented stimulus items. In recent years, however, a fairly standard form of experimental design has been used by those interested in short-term memory. Basically, we present a subject with a set of stimulus items in serial order, one item at a time, for some fixed period of time. After all the items have been presented once, a short period may follow during which he is asked to do some irrelevant task. Then he is given a test to determine his memory of the items.

The purpose of the irrelevant task is to impose a controlled delay between presentation of the stimulus item and its test in order to minimize how much the subject rehearses the items. Typical tasks used in these delay periods include requiring the subject to count backwards rapidly from some arbitrary starting point (often he must count backwards by threes, e.g., 572, 569, 566, . . .) or to name or write things which are presented at a rate which is difficult for him to follow. In many experiments the irrelevant task is eliminated completely and the presentation of later stimulus items acts as an irrelevant task for the retention of the earlier items.

There are a variety of testing procedures that can be used to determine how much a subject remembers about the stimulus list, but they all can be reduced to two basic methods. One, *recall*, is to ask the subject to recite what he remembers of the items shown him, giving him a point for each item that matches one on the stimulus list. The other testing procedure, *recognition*, is to show the subject test items and ask him to decide whether or not they were part of the stimulus list.

These are simplified abstractions of the actual procedures. As might be expected, there are many possible variations: in *free recall*, subjects are allowed to recollect as many items as they can in whatever order they like; in *serial recall*, they must report the items in the same order in which they were presented; in *ordered recall* they can report the items in any order they please, but they must also report the order or position of their presentation; in *probed recall*, the subject is presented with some cue for the proper item, sometimes an associate of the item, sometimes its location in the list, sometimes a neighboring item, and sometimes a portion of the item itself. The list of alternative testing methods which use the recall procedure can be extended indefinitely, with today's list being extended by the ingenuity of tomorrow's experimenter.

The same sort of catalog can be made for recognition tests of memory. The main variations, however, center around two themes: one, the number of tests that a subject is given for each stimulus list, and two, the number of items used per test. Thus, in *simple recognition*, one test item is presented and the subject must decide whether or not it appeared in the list. In *multiple alternative* situations, however, the subject is presented with several test items: his job is to decide which one was presented earlier. A recall test of memory can be considered to be a form of multiple alternative tests of memory whenever the subject knows the set of possible answers.

Let us examine in more detail a typical experiment. We shall use a recognition experiment for illustrative purposes. Such an experiment might proceed as follows: the subject is presented with a list of stimulus items, one item at a time. At the end of the stimulus list, some signal is presented (for example, a high-pitched tone) to indicate the end of the list. Then a test item is presented. The subject knows that either the test item is *old*, having come from any one of the preceding stimulus items, or it is *new*, not having occurred previously in the list. Usually the subject knows the relative frequency with which a test item will be old or new. The subject makes his response by saying *yes* (the item was old) or *no* (the item was not old) and after a delay of a few seconds the whole procedure starts again.

EXPERIMENTAL PROBLEMS

We have talked as if the retention of one list can be isolated from the retention of any other list. This is not true. Most short-term memory experiments are conducted by presenting numerous lists of items to a small number of subjects. The experimenters would prefer to present but one list to one subject and then study the retention of each item on that list. Unfortunately this is not possible, for two rather obvious reasons.

First, it is difficult to get an accurate measure of how much is remembered of one item on a single trial. We can make only crude estimates of the quantity of information retained about an item from a single trial. Sometimes a subject can recall all of an item, sometimes only parts. Other times he can recall all the parts correctly, but in the wrong order. Sometimes he is very confident that his response was correct, other times he guesses. All of these measures are somewhat crude, however, partly because of the lack of precision of our measurements (in measuring the "completeness" of a response, for example) and partly because we lack adequate theories.

The second reason why single lists do not give sufficient information is that, as we have seen in Chapter 4, the act of recalling one item on the list interferes with the memory of the other items. Thus, unless we can invent a technique for measuring the memory strength of all items in memory simultaneously, we are forced to restrict our measures to a single item with each presentation of a list. To get more complete information we need more list presentations.

The standard way of performing these experiments is to present a list of items to a subject, test his retention of an item on the list, and then, after a short pause, repeat the procedure. Many hours of testing are necessary to get sufficient information about the retention of each item.

A single subject may sometimes participate in an experiment for a period of 50 hours, spread out over 25 to 50 sessions during a one or two month period. The repetitive nature of the experiment is important. It is necessary because of the probabilistic nature of the subject's responses: sometimes the subject will remember an item correctly, other times, he will not. To measure the response probability with any accuracy, the experimenter must make 50 to 100 tests of every condition he feels is important. This means that in order to examine the serial position curve for a list with 10 items in it, as many as 1000 lists may have to be presented. Moreover, if the test item is old only 50 percent of the time, it will take 2000 trials to get those 1000 lists. If items are presented at the rate of one each second, the presentation of the 10 item list and its test takes 11 seconds. If we allow 10 seconds for the subject to respond and then a 10 second pause before the next list, the 21,000 items contained in those 2000 lists will take approximately 20 hours to present. And this is just one simple experiment and one subject.

In these experiments we require a peculiar type of behavior on the part of the subject. We ask him to retain as much as he can about each list until the time of test and then, before the new list is presented, he must "forget" what he learned. Were we to present a subject with but one list and measure his retention of that list, we would get different results. In fact, it appears clear that the first few lists tested yield far better retention than do tests of later lists. Once a sufficient number of lists have been presented, repeated tests of lists seem to represent stable measures of performance. Most experimenters discard the results from the first few lists when they analyze their data in order to minimize the effects of this initial period of superior performance.

Aside from the obvious difficulties of getting subjects to do such a lengthy experiment, what does the prolonged nature of these experiments imply about the ways by which they go about doing such a task? All these presentations must certainly have their effect on retention.

Previous experience in experimental tasks is known to reduce the amount of material that can be retained. The effect of previously learned material on current learning is called proactive interference and it cannot be ignored in assessing the results of experiments in short-term memory. In at least one sense, however, this heavy proactive interference is good. To understand this argument, it is first necessary to believe that short- and long-term memories do indeed exist as separate systems. When trying to distinguish between short- and long-term storage one continually faces the problem of separating the effects of these two memory systems. Whenever subjects learn material, both short-term and long-term traces are active and it is a difficult task to determine how much of the performance at the time of test was caused by each factor. Whenever a single subject is tested repeatedly, however, we are almost guaranteed that there will be very little or no long-term retention. The subject has a hard enough time keeping his full attention on the experiment, without also learning the material for long durations of time. It can be argued that if there are really two separate memory systems, one long-term and one short, heavy proactive interference guarantees that only short-term traces will be active at the time of test. The functions which one gets in these experiments may very well be more representative of a pure short-term memory function than results from other experiments in which proactive effects have been held to a minimum.

There is an obvious alternative to the procedure just described in which one subject was presented with 21,000 items. Instead of presenting a single subject with 2000 lists of items, as just described, we could present a large number of subjects each with a few lists. Both techniques have advantages and disadvantages. The first, using a single subject, means that our results come from someone who is very experienced in the experimental task: these results are not necessarily representative of how people normally behave. Moreover, as we have discussed, the act of presenting so much material may change the results we are studying. Finally, how are we to say that the results from a few highly trained subjects are representative of all human beings?

The second technique, using many subjects for few trials, assumes that all the individuals tested are similar to one another, so that the averaged results are typical of the average subject. Unfortunately, we have no guarantee that there is such a thing as an average subject. On the contrary, there are many examples of instances in which average performance is representative of no single individual. When subjects are used for a short period of time, they probably are learning how to perform the task as the experiment progresses. The results will therefore reflect aspects of learning. It is possible to use experimental designs that carefully balance the order in which subjects and conditions are tested so that every experimental condition suffers equally from extra-experimental variables such as learning. These techniques are valuable for some purposes, but bad for others. In particular, they make it difficult to determine what mathematical function governs the results of an experiment because the effects of an unknown (although presumably equal) amount of extraneous variables (noise) have been added to the results.

The technique one uses in running experiments must be determined by the type of question one asks of the results and, to some extent, by personal philosophy. The philosophy in these chapters will be to emphasize studies which use individual subjects studied over long periods of time. This technique is used primarily because we ask questions about the detailed nature of the processes which govern the phenomena of attention and memory. For the issues discussed in this book, the study of individual subjects seems to be the best experimental procedure.

REHEARSAL

Rehearsal is an extremely important part of the act of memorizing and, therefore, ought to be an extremely important part of theories of memory. Unfortunately, we have difficulty in defining what rehearsal is, let alone describing its nature or suggesting how it might work. Rehearsal seems to be silent, inner speech. There is little question that we say things to ourselves in order to help remember them, but how necessary this is for memory and how much else is involved is not known. Most authors tend to be conservative in their statements about rehearsal, leaving open the possibility that it might be conscious or unconscious, audible or subaudible, or all or none of these things. In fact, a common practice seems to be to ignore the whole thing. For example, in the first modern book on memory published in many years (Adams, 1967), the word "rehearsal" does not appear in either the index or the table of contents, although it does show up a few times in the text.

In the previous chapter (Chapter 4), we have seen how George Sperling incorporated subvocal rehearsal into a specific memory mechanism. In future chapters we shall return to a discussion of some of the implications of this vocalization. To anticipate slightly, the vocal aspect of rehearsal implies that material is remembered in auditory form, even when it was originally presented in visual form. For the present chapter, we need simply note that the way in which a subject rehearses can change the results of experiments in memory. If a subject decides to concentrate his rehearsal on the first items of a list, he will remember these better than if they were not rehearsed so extensively. Because psychologists have tended to ignore the existence of rehearsal (more on this topic when we discuss mnemonics in Chapter 6), they have seldom bothered to ask what their subjects were doing. For this reason, when interpreting the results of many experiments in memory, it is necessary to ask how much they are caused by individual idiosyncrasies of the rehearsal strategies of subjects, as opposed to basic processes.

THEORIES OF SHORT-TERM MEMORY

The recent views on the nature of immediate memory is that it represents a temporary storage device which can retain a small, limited amount of material. Almost every designer of modern information processing devices has discovered that it is necessary to have temporary storage units at all places that communicate with the environment (i.e., on all input-output lines). These storage units or buffers are necessary because the mode and speed at which information processes can take place within the device differ from the mode and speed at which information can be received from or transmitted to the environment. The arguments which cause these buffers to be necessary on man-made equipment are very general ones; they apply to anything which attempts to perform logical operations on information received from the environment. Hence, they should apply to living organisms as well as to artificial ones. Of course, logical arguments about the desirability of a mechanism such as short-term memory are certainly not proof of its existence in humans.

If, for the moment, we accept the argument that special short-term memory does exist, we still have to determine its properties. One of the earliest detailed descriptions of the possible operation of a short-term memory was provided by the English psychologist John Brown, in a series of papers published in 1958 and 1959. He suggested that material in this memory fades away in time unless some effort is made to retain it by means of rehearsal. Rehearsal, he argued, maintains an item in short-term memory by renewing the trace of the item in much the same way that a new presentation of that item would revive it. Once the rehearsal ceased, however, the item would decay as if it had just been presented. Thus, in short-term memory, rehearsal served to prolong a trace, but had no other effect. We must assume, however, that rehearsal of an item would also increase its likelihood of being stored permanently, perhaps in a different memory system. This argument was not stressed by Brown, but it would appear to be a logical extension of his theory. In fact, it is needed by almost any theory of memory because, after all, we do remember some items for very long periods of time. Any theorist who proposes a short-term memory model in which all items eventually decay to nonexistence is obviously restricting himself from considering the properties of long-term memory.

John Brown specified two other things in his theory. One point was the nature of decay. The process of decay was considered to be analogous to the process of adding noise to the memory trace. Thus, the image in memory became less and less distinct over time, with a continual decrease in the number of details that could be recovered. Memory errors increase as the image decays, with the incorrectly recalled items bearing some similarity to the original. The other point Brown made was that an unrehearsed memory trace decayed as a result of the passage of time. This point has been much disputed lately, with an opposing view contending that time has little effect on the material stored in memory. It is, of course, very difficult to distinguish a theory which postulates decay in time from one which postulates decay caused by interference, primarily because it is not possible to do the one critical experiment which everyone would accept. The critical experiment would be to present material to a subject, have him do nothing for some period of time, and then test his retention of the items. The interference theorist would predict no loss: the time theorist would predict substantial loss. The catch is that it is not possible for a subject to "do nothing." Rehearsal, thinking, conscious and unconscious processes all occur continually. There is no simple switch we can throw to turn a subject "off" for a short period of time. Who is to say, then, whether any decay in memory is a result of the passage of time or activity?

The rate of forgetting of poorly rehearsed material was demonstrated by Lloyd and Margaret Peterson at Indiana University in 1959. In order to minimize rehearsal, they had their subjects perform a task which was both irrelevant to the memory task and difficult. The task was to count backwards (by threes) from a randomly determined starting point and in time with the rhythm produced by a metronome. The memory task itself was to retain a sequence of three consonant letters. Normally, it is not difficult to retain three letters, but in this experiment, the deterioration was almost complete after 18 seconds.

Rapid decay of material from memory occurs only under limited experimental conditions which include the presence of some interfering (or rehearsal-preventing) task. This suggests that the span of immediate memory is limited primarily by the rehearsal process. A possible memory system is one in which the limited capacity of immediate memory is due to difficulty in rehearsing too many items at once. Rehearsal might serve both to maintain material in immediate memory and help transfer it to a more permanent store. This theory was proposed in 1965 by Nancy C. Waugh and Donald A. Norman, and is stated in the next selection.

PRIMARY MEMORY *

NANCY C. WAUGH and DONALD A. NORMAN

It is a well-established fact that the longest series of unrelated digits, letters, or words that a person can recall verbatim after one presentation seldom exceeds 10 items. It is also true, however, that one can nearly always recall the most recent item in a series, no matter how long the series—but only if this item may be recalled immediately, or if it may be rehearsed during the interval between its presentation and recall. Otherwise it is very likely to be lost. If we may assume that attending to a current item precludes reviewing a prior one, we can say that the span of immediate memory must be limited in large part by our inability to rehearse, and hence retain, the early items in a sequence while attempting to store the later ones. Our limited memory span would then be but one manifestation of our general inability to think about two things at the same time.

Why should an unrehearsed item in a list be forgotten so swiftly? Is its physiological trace in some sense written over by the traces of the items that follow it? Or does this trace simply decay within a brief interval, regardless of how that interval is filled?

— — —

We shall assume here that rehearsal simply denotes the recall of a verbal item—either immediate or delayed, silent or overt, deliberate or involuntary. The initial perception of a stimulus probably must also qualify as a rehearsal. Obviously a very conspicuous item or one that relates easily to what we have already learned can be retained with a minimum of conscious effort. We assume that relatively homogeneous or unfamiliar material must, on the other hand, be deliberately rehearsed if it is to be retained. Actually, we shall not be concerned here with the exact role of rehearsal in the memorization process. We are simply noting that, in the usual verbal-learning experiment, the likelihood that an item in a homogeneous list will be recalled tends to increase with the amount of time available for its rehearsal.

— — —

* Nancy C. Waugh and Donald A. Norman. Primary memory. *Psychol. Rev.*, 1965, **72**, 89, 92–93. Copyright 1965 by the American Psychological Association, and reproduced with their permission.

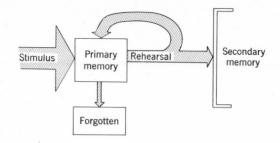

Fig. 2. The primary and secondary memory system. All verbal items enter PM, where they are either rehearsed or forgotten. Rehearsed items may enter SM.

Conversely, material which is not rehearsed is rapidly lost, regardless of the rate at which it is presented. It is as though rehearsal transferred a recently perceived verbal item from one memory store of very limited capacity to another more commodious store from which it can be retrieved at a much later time.

We shall follow James (1890) in using the terms *primary* and *secondary memory* (PM and SM) to denote the two stores. James defined these terms introspectively: an event in PM has never left consciousness and is part of the psychological present, while an event recalled from SM has been absent from consciousness and belongs to the psychological past. PM is a faithful record of events just perceived; SM is full of gaps and distortions. James believed that PM extends over a fixed period of time. We propose instead that it encompasses a certain number of events regardless of the time they take to occur. Our goal is to distinguish operationally between PM and SM on the basis of the model that we shall now describe.

Consider the general scheme illustrated in Fig. 2. Every verbal item that is attended to enters PM. As we have seen, the capacity of this system is sharply limited. New items displace old ones; displaced items are permanently lost. When an item is rehearsed, however, it remains in PM, and it may enter into SM. We should like to assume, for the sake of simplicity, that the probability of its entering SM is independent of its position in a series and of the time at which it is rehearsed. Thus, it would not matter whether the item was rehearsed immediately on entering PM or several seconds later: as long at it was in PM, it would make the transition into SM with fixed probability.

In their discussions, Waugh and Norman place heavy emphasis on the role of rehearsal in prolonging the period of storage of material in primary memory and increasing the likelihood of entry into secondary memory. Rehearsal for grammatical material is both a serial and a verbal process. If rehearsal plays the roles suggested, then it may be the key to the relation between attention and memory. We have seen that when one channel of information is being attended to, little information is retained about the properties of the other channel. Even more striking, when subjects shadow verbal material, they have little retention of the material just shadowed, even though this material must have undergone considerable processing by the nervous system in order for it to be heard and repeated verbally. Could it be that the difficulty of performing the shadowing task precludes the possibility of rehearsal, thus minimizing the longer-term retention of the shadowed material?

The picture just presented of memory makes for nice reading, but is it accurate? It will take a while for the slow process of scientific investigation to reach definitive conclusions, but meanwhile it might be wise to review some of the arguments now going on and mention some of the problems not well-handled by the sensory-primary-secondary division of memory.

One experimental finding that must be explained by any theory of memory is the serial position effect of recall. The serial position effect refers to the fact that when a list of homogeneous items are learned, best retention will occur for the two ends of the list and poorest retention will be in the middle. The exact shape of the serial position curve depends upon a number of experimental variables, but the basic fact that the beginning and end of a list of items show increased retention over the others occurs again and again in a variety of experimental settings. (The serial position curve is discussed in more detail in Chapter 8.)

The relative superiority of items at the end of the list (recent items and, hence, the recency effect) over those at the middle can be accounted for by the primary memory phenomenon. When the list has just been presented, the last items are still in primary memory and can be recalled immediately. Even if immediate recall of last items is prevented, they may still be rehearsed. Since, by definition, no items are presented after the last one, the rehearsal tends to be prolonged and effective. If both immediate recall and rehearsal of the last items of a list are prevented, the recency effect ought to disappear, and indeed it does.

Early items in a list also receive superior recall, and this effect cannot be explained as simply as the recency effect. Waugh and Norman simply ignored the problem by restricting their analysis to items beyond the first few. Knowledge does not come through ignorance, however, and it is clear that eventually the phenomenon will have to be explained. A possible explanation, compatible with the multiple memory assumption, is that early items in a list received increased attention over later ones and, hence, are more likely to be transferred to longer-term memory systems. By this notion, therefore, the serial position effect in short-term memory experiments is due to increased attention of early items and the easy recall of late items from primary memory. The evidence necessary to support the theory comes from the fact that it is possible to modify the shape of the serial position curve dramatically simply by instructing the subject how he should spend his time. We can flatten the initial part of the curve by asking the subject to spend "equal amounts of attention on each item." ("Think about each item when it is presented; when a new item is presented, concentrate on it. Do not think of any of the earlier items.") It is also possible to enhance the memory of the first item by suitable instructions. ("Concentrate all your attention on the first item, even while the other items are being presented.")

A second theory suggests that transfer from primary to secondary storage is performed by an attention or rehearsal mechanism that can handle only one item at a time. The first item presented in a list automatically receives full attention of the processor. The second and later items must wait until the first item has finished. A queue is formed of items waiting for transfer into longer-term memories. Items toward the end of the list have an increasing probability of being forgotten before their turn comes up.

A different type of theoretical explanation of the increased retention of early items is that of proactive interference. The experimental finding is simple: retention decreases with the number of similar *previous* tasks. The normal explanations for proactive interference are based on an interference theory in which memory traces from earlier learned material become confused with traces from material presently being learned. Early items in a list suffer least from proactive interference effects.

HOW MANY MEMORIES?

A common argument against the existence of several different types of memories is that similar laws apply to phenomena attributed to different systems. The same serial position effect is noticed in studies of short-term memory as in studies of long-term memory, the same type of proactive interference, the same relationship between similarity of items and ease of retention, and the same relationships, in fact, for a long list of psychological phenomena. These similarities of behavior can be taken to imply that there is but one type of memory, with perhaps different modes of excitation. What we have been calling sensory memory may simply represent a rapid decay of traces in the memory; what we have been calling primary memory may be a somewhat slower decay of the traces in the memory; and what we have been calling secondary memory might be an even slower decay of the same memory. In fact, one of the parameters of memory might simply be the rate at which stored information is dissipated. According to this argument, then, we are mistaken when we attempt to attribute different rates of decay to different memory systems.

Waugh and Norman were aware of this controversy and they responded in this way: [3]

DISCUSSION

We should at this point like to consider the general question of whether all verbal information is stored in the same system or whether, as we have assumed here, there are two independent mnemonic processes that contribute to retention even over very short intervals. The proponents of a unitary theory of memory, eloquently led by Melton (1963), have argued that recall after a few seconds is affected in very similar ways by the variables that govern recall over much longer intervals; and that therefore the distinction between a short-term memory mechanism, on the one hand, and a longer term mechanism, on the other, is purely arbitrary. The following facts have been cited in support of this argument:

1. Short-term retention improves, just as does long-term retention, when the material to be recalled is repeated before a test of retention, or when it is repeated between successive tests (Hebb, 1961; Hellyer, 1962).

2. Retention after a brief delay is subject to proactive interference, as is retention after a long delay (Keppel and Underwood, 1962; Loess, 1964). Why, asks the unitary theorist, should we distinguish between short- and long-term retention if we cannot find any quantitative and experimentally manipulatable differences between them? This question might well be disturbing if one took the position that the two processes have sharply defined non-overlapping temporal boundaries such that items recalled within some critical interval after their initial occurrence must have been retrieved from one system, whereas items recalled beyond this interval must have been retrieved from another. (Such a view would imply, interestingly enough, that an item would have to remain in a short-term storage for some specified number of seconds before passing into longer term storage, if it did so at all.)

But what if we do not require that the two systems be mutually exclusive? Then the probability that an item will be recalled will depend on both the

[3] Waugh and Norman, Primary memory. *Op. cit.* Pages 100–102.

probability that it is still in PM and the probability that it has entered into SM in the interval between its presentation and the start of the interfering sequence (or even during this sequence, if the subject is able to rehearse). All those variables that determine the likelihood of recalling a given item from SM—such as its position in a closely spaced series of tests, or the number of times it has been repeated—will then determine the observed proportion recalled after a brief interval. We believe we have shown, however, that the likelihood of recalling an item from PM depends only upon how far it was from the end of the list, quite independent of whether or not it was also in SM; and we submit that most of the published data on short-term retention actually reflect the properties of both memory systems.

We would like to make one final point: the existence of some rather compelling introspective evidence in favor of two distinct mnemonic systems. PM, as we have defined it here, is best illustrated by a person's ability to recall verbatim the most recent few words in a sentence that he is hearing or speaking, even when he is barely paying attention to what is being said, or to what he is saying. Given that the flow of speech is intelligible, failures in the immediate recall of words we have just heard—errors of either omission, transposition, or substitution—are probably so rare as to be abnormal. Indeed, we believe that it would be impossible to understand or to generate a grammatical utterance if we lacked this rather remarkable mnemonic capacity. In order to recall a sentence verbatim at a later time, however, we usually have to rehearse it while it is still available in PM.

The same effect holds for meaningless arrangements of verbal items. If we present a subject with a random string of words, letters, or digits, and ask him to reproduce them in any order he chooses, he can maximize the number he recalls by "unloading" the last few items immediately. Most subjects in free-recall experiments report that these very late items tend to be lost if they are not recalled immediately, whereas items that came earlier in the list can be retrieved at leisure, if they can be recalled at all. In the colorful terminology of one such subject (Waugh, 1961), the most recent items in a verbal series reside temporarily in a kind of "echo box," from which they can be effortlessly parroted back. When an experienced subject is trying to memorize a list of serial items, moreover, he "fills up" successive echo boxes as the list is read to him and attempts to rehearse the contents of each. He will invariably lose some items if rehearsal is delayed too long or if he attempts to load his echo box with more items than it can hold. We think it very likely that the PM function describes the (variable) capacity of this mechanism. We would remind you in this connection that, within very broad limits, the rate at which someone is speaking does not affect your ability to follow his words—just as differences in the rate at which meaningless lists of digits are presented do not exert any profound effect on the PM function.

CONCLUSIONS

We have tried to demonstrate the existence of a short-term or PM system that is independent of any longer term or secondary store by showing that one function relating probability of recall to number of intervening items can describe a number of seemingly disparate sets of experimental results. In doing so, we have deliberately avoided discussing a number of problems raised in our analyses. Foremost in our list of problems is the definition of an item. Certainly the idea of a discrete verbal unit is crucial to our theory. The interference effect that we have studied seems to be invariant over a broad class of units and combinations of units—single digits, nonsense trigrams, and meaningful words. How long a string of such primitive units can we combine and still have one item? Is an item determined by our grammatical habits? Is it determined by the duration of the verbal stimulus? Is it determined by both? We do not know.

We have also avoided discussing the possible rules whereby items now in PM are displaced by later items. Are items lost independently of one another, or do they hang and fall together? It may perhaps prove difficult to answer this question experimentally, but it should not be impossible.

Finally, at what stage in the processing of incoming information does our PM reside? Is it in the peripheral sensory mechanism? Probably not. The work of Sperling (1960) indicates that "sensory memory"—to use Peterson's (1963) phrase—decays within a matter of milliseconds, whereas we have dealt in our analysis with retention intervals on the order of seconds. Does storage in PM precede the attachment of meaning to discrete verbal stimuli? Must a verbal stimulus be transformed into an auditory image in order to be stored in PM, even if it was presented visually? We refer the reader to a recent paper by Sperling (1963) for some thoughts on the latter question.

We close the chapter at this point, not because the issues have been resolved, but because almost all that can be said has been said. To do more, we need more evidence. It will take a new type of experiment to be able to resolve the differences among these experimental controversies. Whether the eventual resolution will be a compromise of positions or an entirely new view of memory cannot yet be said.

The natural progression of topics would lead us next to a consideration of secondary memory. Yet, in spite of all the years of research on problems in memory, even less is known about the mechanisms which underlie secondary memory than those of primary memory. As a result, although we now switch our discussion to the study of secondary memory, we do it differently from the way primary memory was treated. First we move to a study of the rules of organization by which information is put in and retrieved from secondary memory. Then (in Chapter 7) we investigate how things are stored.

SUGGESTED READINGS

The discussions presented in this chapter are all heavily biased toward the point of view that the memory system is one part of the overall process of dealing with information and that it is sensible to distinguish between primary and secondary (or short- and long-term) stages of memory. In order to understand the controversy on these points, see the more balanced presentation in the recent book on human memory by Jack Adams (1967), especially Chapters 3 and 5. Adams reviews the arguments presented by the proponents of all the various viewpoints, giving approximately equal weight to all sides. Further elaboration on the conventional arguments can be found in several places: in the symposiums edited by Cofer (1961), Cofer and Musgrave (1963), and Melton (1964), and in the collection of reprints edited by Slamecka (1967), especially the papers by Melton (1963) and Keppel and Underwood (1962). See also the discussion of the readings suggested for Chapter 6 (page 123).

Further arguments along the lines of this chapter will be given in Chapter 8. In addition, a further series of studies have expanded the arguments supporting primary memory: Norman (1966), Norman and Waugh (1968), and Waugh and Norman (1968). Moreover, in the paper on attention (discussed in Chapter 2, Fig. 2), I have argued that although the primary and secondary memories are indeed separate logical elements with different temporal properties, they may in fact share the same physical structure (Norman, 1968).

Neisser (1967, Chapter 9) takes a different approach to the whole problem of primary memory (he calls it "active verbal memory"), by treating it as "a manifestation of auditory synthesis extended over time." The interested reader had best read the entire chapter.

The student who wishes to learn more about information theory will find that both Arbib (1964) and Raisbeck (1963) provide very readable introductions. Arbib, in particular, is concerned with issues closely related to those discussed in this book. An interesting and novel approach to memory and related areas from the point of view of an Electrical Engineer can be found in the book by S. Deutsch (1967).

Papers on memory are usually found in the following experimental journals:

British Journal of Psychology
Journal of Experimental Psychology
Journal of Verbal Learning and Verbal Behavior
Psychological Review
Psychonomic Science
Quarterly Journal of Experimental Psychology

6

Mnemonics

THROUGHOUT the centuries man has been concerned with the practical art of memory. Everyone knows that normally it is difficult to memorize things. Yet a few people have always known special techniques that make the task possible with apparent ease. We tend to ignore these techniques today because they are mere tricks and sophistry—the practitioners exhibit themselves as stage entertainers or advertise themselves and their methods in unrespectable classified advertisements—but we cannot deny that the techniques work. In fact, we ought to examine procedures that simplify the job of memorizing with great care. Not only might they be useful in our lives, but the secrets of those who practice the art of memory ought to shed some light on the organization and operation of the mechanisms involved in memory. Certainly the things one must do in order to learn material easily bear some relationship to the way that information processes operate.

In this chapter we examine some of the popular systems for improving one's memory. First, we question the common notion that memory is simply a skill that improves with practice. Then, we move to the study of the principles which underlie techniques for efficient memorization. Some of these principles come from the literature of experimental psychology, but most come from the popular proponents of various memory systems. Finally, we conclude by examining what little is known about the plans and organization of memory and by speculating on the nature of the psychological principles which lie behind the operations of the popular memory systems.

The study of methods for improving memory has long been popular, for a good memory can serve its owner well in many activities. Who among us has not wished for better ability to retain important material?

Through the years a number of systems have been developed for the purpose of improving memory. The details of the systems are not always known, for often their designer has kept them secret, hoping to gain either an advantage over his competitors or wealth from his students. But a study of most public systems (and guesses about the techniques used by practitioners of secret systems) indicates that they all have similar bases: they teach the user to pay attention and to learn how to organize.

Through their experiments, psychologists have unearthed a number of principles which underlie the retention of material. One of the first results of these studies was a negative finding: the debunking of the notion that memory is a skill in the sense that weightlifting is. It used to be thought (and indeed, by some people, still is) that if one wants a good memory (or good muscles) one simply practices memorization (or lifting weights). The most positive stand against this idea seems to have been taken by William James who spent 5 pages of his textbook denouncing the notion that exercises in memory strengthens the capacity to memorize. Indeed, James was so moved by the force of his own arguments that he did, what was for him, a very unusual thing: he did an experiment. He laboriously trained himself daily in the learning of poetry "by heart." For 8 consecutive days he learned 158 lines of Victor Hugo's *Satyr*. Then he spent 38 days learning the entire first book of *Paradise Lost*. All this effort, James thought, should have tremendously improved his memory. But when he went back to Victor Hugo, he found that an additional 158 lines took him, if anything, longer to learn than the first set of 158 lines. Apparently no good had resulted from his efforts. Not trusting these results, James set out to test a whole series of surprisingly docile friends who spent many weeks learning many lines of poetry and found, on the whole, no improvement in their ability to learn material after all their labor.

Studies of the effect of performance in one task upon learning or performance in another task are called studies in transfer. Thus, James' experiments on memory training can be considered experiments on transfer of memory skill. Although James was correct in his conclusion that practice alone does not improve one's ability to memorize, he was a bit premature in concluding that it is all wasted effort. It turns out that it is possible to learn techniques which considerably improve the skills of memory. But practice is useless unless you know the rules. For example, it helps considerably to form rhymes and to form images and associations among the items to be learned. It helps also to relax and have confidence in one's own ability to memorize.

In 1927, Woodrow repeated James' experiment, only with more care.

He wanted to see what improvement in memorization would come about after practice in "proper methods of memorizing." He found that a group of students who simply practiced memorizing lists for several hours did no better than a control group of students who did not practice. This verified the conclusion reached by James. But a group of students who were instructed in proper techniques of memorizing did much better after the same amount of study. Thus in memory, as in most things, sheer blind practice is of little or no use; informed learning of a set of rules and techniques does prove useful.

OUR IGNORANCE OF MNEMONICS

Psychologists have tended to avoid the study of aids to memory. There are a number of reasons for this. Primarily, it has been assumed that these aids offered no new techniques, only clever utilizations of old ones. Certainly the uncontrolled use of these tricks complicate the normal experiment in learning or memory, for each experimental subject applies them differently making it very difficult to interpret the results. Thus, experimenters have tried to eliminate the use of such memory systems, either by instruction or by designing the experiments so that such techniques are difficult to apply successfully.

The problem that confronts us, then, is that on the one hand psychologists have studied the various factors that go into the formation and retention of simple associations in rote memory tasks; on the other hand, people are poorest at learning things by rote memory, instead they use tricks, gimmicks, and mnemonics to transform the nonsense of the psychologist into the sense that they find easiest to remember. As a result, all we have to go on in our description of what subjects actually do is a collection of anecdotes rather than firm experimental evidence. This has one virtue, however: anecdotes are much more interesting to read than the articles in the *Journal of Experimental Psychology*.

Before we conclude too readily that psychologists in the first half of the 20th century were horrible ogres, holding back the progress of knowledge, let us look at their position for a minute. For one thing, are we not guilty of the same procedures when, in our study of primary memory, we warned subjects to avoid rehearsal, presented dull, meaningless material for hours and hours, and in general, avoided anything which might allow the subjects to retain the material which we were presenting? The answer must be yes, so either we are hypocrites or there are valid reasons for trying to eliminate the clever strategies of subjects.

Perhaps the point can best be made by examining the primary memory studies. Our underlying notion is that all individuals have a common, limited capacity storage process. This is the process which we are interested in studying but, obviously, it is a memory which by itself can be of little use in our everyday performance. People use various procedures to get material which they consider important from this limited primary memory into a more commodious secondary memory. As a result, any effective memorization procedure will only confound us when we try to determine the structure of primary memory. We can hardly study how material is forgotten from primary memory if our subjects are able to retain it in secondary memory. So we do our best to insure that our subjects cannot make use of their normal processes of memorization.

The argument is not too much different for studies of long-term memory. It is true that subjects do their best learning when they are allowed to group, organize, and distort the material they are presented. These mnemonic tricks are useful and maybe even essential to the memory process. The real question, however, is whether there is any essential difference between the basic properties underlying the use of mnemonics and the dull, dreary rote learning that is studied in the laboratory. Most psychologists think not.

It is very difficult to study mnemonic techniques. Subjects have discovered various idiosyncratic procedures which they themselves are often incapable of describing. With little consistency in the use of these mnemonics, performance in the laboratory looks haphazard and erratic: there appears to be no law governing what is retained and what is forgotten. But if mnemonics are truly composed of organized components of rote learning, we would do well first to dissect the rote learning process itself and then, when we understand the basic components of learning and memory, describe how they are used in actual, out-of-the-laboratory situations. The trouble with this rationalization is that it is unproved. It may very well be that the mnemonics offer nothing new for the experimental psychologist, efficient though they may be for the user. But until we investigate them we cannot say for certain that mnemonic techniques are in fact equivalent to a fancy packaging of well-known memory aids.

AN ANECDOTE

One hint that mnemonic techniques might not be related in any simple way to simple associations has been offered by a critical trio of psychologists George Miller, Eugene Galanter and Karl Pribram in their book *Plans and the Structure of Behavior*. In this book, Miller, Galanter and Pribram argued that the human organism consists of a hierarchical organization of flexible decision units. They introduced an important new basic concept, the Plan, which they defined as "any hierarchical process in the organism that can control the order in which sequence of operations is to be performed." A Plan is, for an organism, essentially the same as a program is for a computer. Plans are quite novel in psychological theories and, as yet, poorly understood. The way that Plans enter into the process of remembering is illustrated in these excerpts from Chapter 10 of Miller, Galanter and Pribram.

PLANS FOR REMEMBERING *

GEORGE MILLER, EUGENE GALANTER and KARL PRIBRAM

The usual approach to the study of memorization is to ask how the material is engraved on the nervous system, how the connections between the parts of it become learned, or imprinted, or strengthened, or conditioned. The usual answers have to do with the amount of practice, with the beneficent consequences of success, with the facilitating or inhibiting effects arising from similarity among parts of the materials or between these materials and others, with the meaningfulness or other sources of transfer of previous learning, and so on. No one who knew the experimental data would question that all these factors are important in determining how fast and how well a person will be able to commit a particular string of symbols to memory. The reason for returning to this well-cultivated plot and trying to crowd in another crop is that an important aspect of the memorizing process seems to have been largely ignored.

— — —

A memorizer's task in the psychological laboratory is to learn how to produce a particular sequence of noises that he would never make ordinarily, that have no significance, and that will be of no use to him later. Rote serial memorization is a complicated, tricky thing to learn to do, and when it is mastered it represents a rather special skill. The argument here is that such

* George Miller, Eugene Galanter and Karl Pribram. *Plans and the structure of behavior*. New York: Holt, Rinehart and Winston, 1960. Pages 125, 128–129, 134–136. Copyright 1960 by Holt, Rinehart and Winston. With permission of the publisher.

a skill could not run itself off successfully unless it were guided in its execution by a Plan of the sort we have been discussing. What the subject is telling us when he reports all the wild and improbable connections he had to use is the way in which he developed a Plan to control his performance during the test period.

Now, it would be extremely easy at this point for us to become confused between two different kinds of Plans that are involved in rote memorization. On the one hand, the subject is attempting to construct a Plan that will, when executed, generate the nonsense syllables in the correct order. But at the same time he must adopt a Plan to guide his memorizing, he must choose a strategy for constructing the Plan for recall. There are a variety of ways open to the subject for memorizing. One is to translate the nonsense syllables into words, then to organize the words into sentences and/or images, even, if necessary, to organize the sentences and images into a story if the length of the list demands such higher-order planning. Another Plan the person can use is sheer drill without any translation, perhaps aided by rhythmic grouping, until the list rolls out as the letters of the alphabet do. Or he can play tricks with imagery—imagining each syllable at a different location in the room, then simply looking there and "reading" it when it is needed, etc. There are a variety of such strategies for learning, and they should be investigated. But it is the impression of the present authors that the average person, when confronted with a list of nonsense syllables for the first time, will do something similar to the performance described above.

Unless a person has some kind of Plan for learning, nothing happens. Subjects have read nonsense syllables hundreds of times and learned almost nothing about them if they were not aware that they would later be tested for recall. In order to get the list memorized, a subject must have that mysterious something called an "intent to learn." Given the intention, the act follows by a steady, slow heave of the will.

— — —

The antagonistic attitude of experimental psychologists toward mnemonic devices is even more violent than their attitude toward their subject's word associations; mnemonic devices are immoral tricks suitable only for evil gypsies and stage magicians. As a result of this attitude almost nothing is known by psychologists about the remarkable feats of memory that are so easily performed when you have a Plan ready in advance. Anecdotes do not contribute to science, of course, but they sometimes facilitate communication—so we shall lapse momentarily into a thoroughly unscientific vein.

One evening we were entertaining a visiting colleague, a social psychologist of broad interests, and our discussion turned to Plans. "But exactly what is a Plan?" he asked. "How can you say that *memorizing* depends on Plans?"

"We'll show you," we replied. "Here is a Plan that you can use for memorizing. Remember first that:

one is a bun,
two is a shoe,
three is a tree,
four is a door,
five is a hive,
six are sticks,
seven is heaven,
eight is a gate,
nine is a line, and
ten is a hen."

"You know, even though it is only ten-thirty here, my watch says one-thirty. I'm really tired, and I'm sure I'll ruin your experiment."

"Don't worry, we have no real stake in it." We tightened our grip on his lapel. "Just relax and remember the rhyme. Now you have part of the Plan. The second part works like this: when we tell you a word, you must form a ludicrous or bizarre association with the first word in your list, and so on with the ten words we recite to you."

"Really, you know, it'll never work. I'm awfully tired," he replied.

"Have no fear," we answered, "just remember the rhyme and then form the association. Here are the words:

1. ashtray,
2. firewood,
3. picture,
4. cigarette,
5. table,
6. matchbook,
7. glass,
8. lamp,
9. shoe,
10. phonograph."

The words were read one at a time, and after reading the word, we waited until he announced that he had the association. It took about five seconds on the average to form the connection. After the seventh word he said that he was sure the first six were already forgotten. But we persevered.

After one trial through the list, we waited a minute or two so that he could collect himself and ask any questions that came to mind. Then we said, "What is number eight?"

He stared blankly, and then a smile crossed his face, "I'll be damned," he said. "It's 'lamp.' "

"And what number is cigarette?"

He laughed outright now, and then gave the correct answer.

"And there is no strain," he said, "absolutely no sweat."

We proceeded to demonstrate that he could in fact name every word correctly, and then asked, "Do you think that memorizing consists of piling up increments of response strength that accumulate as the words are repeated?" The question was lost in his amazement.

Call them what you will—plans, tricks, mnemonics—it is clear that they aid memory. Let us examine some of these tricks in more detail and see what we can make of them. To do so, we must leave experimental psychology and go to the advertisements in magazines, to second-hand book stores, and to other, similar, sources of literature. Popular writings on mnemonics must be our primary source of information because, as we have seen, the professional literature has carefully avoided the whole area. There are hundreds of books on methods for improving one's memory. They differ mainly in the skill with which they are written and the dogmatism with which their "secrets" are presented. But, though it is easy to sneer at their style, it is not wise to deny their content.

MNEMONIC TECHNIQUES

A comparison of the many techniques for improving memory which are offered by the various proponents shows that everyone's system seems to have much in common with everyone else's. In fact, the prevalence of common features makes us suspect that there might really be something to these methods, although the search through the literature of memory systems is something like a search through the literature of the alchemists for the recipe for gunpowder. The alchemist tells us that the secret is the powdered frog's tongue (gathered by the light of the full moon). But if we look carefully, we can also discover some charcoal, sulphur, and saltpeter. Let us see if we can do the same with mnemonic techniques. All mnemonic devices try to relate the material to be learned to some previously learned organizational scheme. There are many ways that this relation can be established in principle, but, in practice, there is heavy reliance upon but a few standard techniques.

RHYMES

Metrical mnemonics are popular, for they let us connect items which otherwise seem wholly unrelated into a rythmical pattern. Rhymes are particularly good at establishing order relations, for when it is well-constructed, any mistake in the order of recall of the items destroys the rhyme. Thus we find rhyme used when the difficulty in memorization centers around the difficulty of learning the proper ordering.

> *I before e*
> *except after c*

or

> *Thirty days hath September,*
> *April, June and November*

Obviously, in these examples it is not difficult to learn the two letters *i* and *e* or the fact that of the 12 months, one has 28 days, some 30, and some 31. The difficulty comes in remembering the order and exact association among the items. The rhymes establish a rule of organization that is easy to learn and apply. In a sense, rhymes (like most mnemonic devices) serve their purpose too well: one who relies on rhymes finds it difficult to remember one particular thing (say, how many days hath October?) without recalling the rhyme in its entirety.

METHOD OF LOCI

One peculiar method, but a surprisingly powerful one, is to imagine that the various items which are to be learned are located in different physical locations (loci). Recall is accomplished by visualizing each location and, thereby, discovering the object. "Thus, if it were desired to fix in the memory the date of the invention of printing (1436), an imaginary book, or some other symbol of printing, would be placed in the thirty-sixth quadrate or memory-place of the fourth room of the first house of the historic district of the town" (Mitchell, 1910).

The history of the method of loci is presented in a recent book by the English historian, Frances A. Yates, entitled *The Art of Memory*. The use of mnemonic techniques have played an important role in the development of philosophy and architecture from the time of the Greek civilization to Elizabethan England. Although the method has a long history, it seems to have been presented best in its original form, first as an anecdote about the Greek poet Simonides and then as a formal system in the very first textbooks. The basic method of loci is described by Yates in the opening pages of *The Art of Memory*.

THE GREEK ART OF MEMORY *

FRANCES A. YATES

At a banquet given by a nobleman of Thessaly named Scopas, the poet Simonides of Ceos chanted a lyric poem in honour of his host but including a passage in praise of Castor and Pollux. Scopas meanly told the poet that he would only pay him half the sum agreed upon for the panegyric and that he must obtain the balance from the twin gods to whom he had devoted half the poem. A little later, a message was brought in to Simonides that two young men were waiting outside who wished to see him. He rose from the banquet and went out but could find no one. During his absence the roof of the banqueting hall fell in, crushing Scopas and all the guests to death beneath the ruins; the corpses were so mangled that the relatives who came to take them away for burial were unable to identify them. But Simonides remembered the places at which they had been sitting at the table and was therefore able to indicate to the relatives which were their dead. The invisible callers, Castor and Pollux, had handsomely paid for their share in the panegyric by drawing Simonides away from the banquet just before the crash. And this experience suggested to the poet the principles of the art of memory of which he is said to have been the inventor. Noting that it was through his memory of the places at which the guests had been sitting that he had been able to identify the bodies, he realised that orderly arrangement is essential for good memory.

He inferred that persons desiring to train this faculty (of memory) must select places and form mental images of the things they wish to remember and store those images in the places, so that the order of the places will preserve the order of the things, and the images of the things will denote the things themselves, and we shall employ the places and images respectively as a wax writing-tablet and the letters written on it. [1]

The vivid story of how Simonides invented the art of memory is told by Cicero in his De oratore when he is discussing memory as one of the five parts of rhetoric; the story introduces a brief description of the mnemonic of places and images (loci and imagines) which was used by the Roman rhetors.

[1] Cicero. De oratore, II, lxxxvi. Pages 351–4. (See Cicero, 1942.)

Two other descriptions of the classical mnemonic, besides the one given by Cicero, have come down to us, both also in treatises on rhetoric when memory as a part of rhetoric is being discussed; one is in the anonymous *Ad C. Herennium libri IV*; the other is in Quintilian's *Institutio oratoria*.[2]

The first basic fact which the student of the history of the classical art of memory must remember is that the art belonged to rhetoric as a technique by which the orator could improve his memory, which would enable him to deliver long speeches from memory with unfailing accuracy. And it was as a part of the art of rhetoric that the art of memory travelled down through the European tradition in which it was never forgotten, or not forgotten until comparatively modern times, that those infallible guides in all human activities, the ancients, had laid down rules and precepts for improving the memory.

It is not difficult to get hold of the general principles of the mnemonic. The first step was to imprint on the memory a series of *loci* or places. The commonest, though not the only, type of mnemonic place system used was the architectural type. The clearest description of the process is that given by Quintilian.[3] In order to form a series of places in memory, he says, a building is to be remembered, as spacious and varied a one as possible, the forecourt, the living room, bedrooms, and parlours, not omitting statues and other ornaments with which the rooms are decorated. The images by which the speech is to be remembered—as an example of these Quintilian says one may use an anchor or a weapon—are then placed in imagination on the places which have been memorised in the building. This done, as soon as the memory of the facts requires to be revived, all these places are visited in turn and the various deposits demanded of their custodians. We have to think of the ancient orator as moving in imagination through his memory building *whilst* he is making his speech, drawing from the memorised places the images he has placed on them. The method ensures that the points are remembered in the right order, since the order is fixed by the sequence of places in the building.

— — —

In what follows I attempt to give the content of the memory section of *Ad Herennium*, emulating the brisk style of the author, but with pauses for reflection about what he is telling us.

The artificial memory is established from places and images (*Constat igitur artificiosa memoria ex locis et imaginibus*), the stock definition to be forever

[2] The translations used here come from the Loeb edition of the classics, in particular, *Rhetorica ad Herennium* (1954), Cicero (1942), and Quintilianus (1921). Yates has sometimes modified the translations. "In the direction of literalness, particularly in repeating the actual terminology of the mnemonic rather than in using periphrases of the terms." (Yates, 1966, p. 1.)

[3] Quintilianus. *Institutio Oratoria*, XI, ii. Pages 17–22.

repeated down the ages. A *locus* is a place easily grasped by the memory, such as a house, an intercolumnar space, a corner, an arch, or the like. Images are forms, marks or simulacra (*formae, notae, simulacra*) of what we wish to remember. For instance if we wish to recall the genus of a horse, of a lion, of an eagle, we must place their images on definite *loci*.

The art of memory is like an inner writing. Those who know the letters of the alphabet can write down what is dictated to them and read out what they have written. Likewise those who have learned mnemonics can set in places what they have heard and deliver it from memory. "For the places are very much like wax tablets or papyrus, the images like the letters, the arrangement and disposition of the images like the script, and the delivery is like the reading."

If we wish to remember much material we must equip ourselves with a large number of places. It is essential that the places should form a series and must be remembered in their order, so that we can start from any *locus* in the series and move either backwards or forwards from it. If we should see a number of our acquaintances standing in a row, it would not make any difference to us whether we should tell their names beginning with the person standing at the head of the line or at the foot or in the middle. So with memory *loci*. "If these have been arranged in order, the result will be that, reminded by the images, we can repeat orally what we have committed to the *loci*, proceeding in either direction from any *locus* we please."

The formation of the *loci* is of the greatest importance, for the same set of *loci* can be used again and again for remembering different material. The images which we have placed on them for remembering one set of things fade and are effaced when we make no further use of them. But the *loci* remain in the memory and can be used again by placing another set of images for another set of material. The *loci* are like the wax tablets which remain when what is written on them has been effaced and are ready to be written on again.

In order to make sure that we do not err in remembering the order of the *loci* it is useful to give each fifth *locus* some distinguishing mark. We may for example mark the fifth *locus* with a golden hand, and place in the tenth the image of some acquaintance whose name is Decimus. We can then go on to station other marks on each succeeding fifth *locus*.

It is better to form one's memory *loci* in a deserted and solitary place for crowds of passing people tend to weaken the impressions. Therefore the student intent on acquiring a sharp and well-defined set of *loci* will choose an unfrequented building in which to memorise places.

Memory *loci* should not be too much like one another, for instance too many intercolumnar spaces are not good, for their resemblance to one another will be confusing. They should be of moderate size, not too large for this renders the images placed on them vague, and not too small for then an arrangement of images will be overcrowded. They must not be too brightly lighted for then the images placed on them will glitter and dazzle; nor must they be too dark or the shadows will obscure the images. The intervals between the *loci* should be of moderate extent, perhaps about thirty feet, "for like the external eye, so the inner eye of thought is less powerful when you have moved the object of sight too near or too far away."

A person with a relatively large experience can easily equip himself with as many suitable *loci* as he pleases, and even a person who thinks that he does not possess enough sufficiently good *loci* can remedy this. "For thought can embrace any region whatsoever and in it and at will construct the setting of some locus." (That is to say, mnemonics can use what were afterwards called "fictitious places," in contrast to the "real places" of the ordinary method.)

Pausing for reflection at the end of rules for places I would say that what strikes me most about them is the astonishing visual precision which they imply. In a classically trained memory the space between the *loci* can be measured, the lighting of the *loci* is allowed for. And the rules summon up a vision of a forgotten social habit. Who is that man moving slowly in the lonely building, stopping at intervals with an intent face? He is a rhetoric student forming a set of memory *loci*.

"Enough has been said of places," continues the author of *Ad Herennium*, "now we turn to the theory of images." Rules for images now begin, the first of which is that there are two kinds of images, one for "things" (*res*), the other for "words" (*verba*). That is to say "memory for things" makes images to remind of an argument, a notion, or a "thing"; but "memory for words" has to find images to remind of every single word.

I interrupt the concise author here for a moment in order to remind the reader that for the rhetoric student "things" and "words" would have an absolutely precise meaning in relation to the five parts of the rhetoric. Those five parts are defined by Cicero as follows:

> Invention is the excogitation of true things (*res*), or things similar to truth to render one's cause plausible; disposition is the arrangement in order of the things thus discovered; elocution is the accomodation of suitable words to the invented (things); memory is the firm perception in the soul of things and words; pronunciation is the moderating of the voice and body to suit the dignity of the things and words. [4]

"Things" are thus the subject matter of the speech; "words" are the language in which that subject matter is clothed. Are you aiming at an artificial memory to remind you only of the order of the notions, arguments, "things" of your speech? Or do you aim at memorising every single word in it in the right

---

[4] Cicero. *De inventione*, I, vii, 9. (See Cicero, 1949.) Translation made more literal in reproducing *res* and *verba*.

order? The first kind of artificial memory is *memoria rerum;* the second kind is *memoria verborum.* The ideal, as defined by Cicero in the above passage, would be to have a "firm perception in the soul" of both things and words. But "memory for words" is much harder than "memory for things"; the weaker brethren among the author of *Ad Herennium*'s rhetoric students evidently rather jibbed at memorising an image for every single word, and even Cicero himself, as we shall see later, allowed that "memory for things" was enough.

To return to the rules for images. We have already been given the rules for places, what kind of places to choose for memorising. What are the rules about what kind of images to choose for memorising on the places? We now come to one of the most curious and surprising passages in the treatise, namely the psychological reasons which the author gives for the choice of mnemonic images. Why is it, he asks, that some images are so strong and sharp and so suitable for awakening memory, whilst others are so weak and feeble that they hardly stimulate memory at all? We must enquire into this so as to know which images to avoid and which to seek.

Now nature herself teaches us what we should do. When we see in every day life things that are petty, ordinary, and banal, we generally fail to remember them, because the mind is not being stirred by anything novel or marvellous. But if we see or hear something exceptionally base, dishonourable, unusual, great, unbelievable, or ridiculous, that we are likely to remember for a long time. Accordingly, things immediate to our eye or ear we commonly forget; incidents of our childhood we often remember best. Nor could this be so for any other reason than that ordinary things easily slip from the memory while the striking and the novel stay longer in the mind. A sunrise, the sun's course, a sunset are marvellous to no one because they occur daily. But solar eclipses are a source of wonder because they occur seldom, and indeed are more marvellous than lunar eclipses, because these are more frequent. Thus nature shows that she is not aroused by the common ordinary event, but is moved by a new or striking occurrence. Let art, then, imitate nature, find what she desires, and follow as she directs. For in invention nature is never last, education never first; rather the beginnings of things arise from natural talent, and the ends are reached by discipline.

We ought, then, to set up images of a kind that can adhere longest in memory. And we shall do so if we establish similitudes as striking as possible; if we set up images that are not many or vague but active (*imagines agentes*); if we assign to them exceptional beauty or singular ugliness; if we ornament some of them, as with crowns or purple cloaks, so that the similitude may be more distinct to us; or if we somehow disfigure them, as by introducing one stained with blood or soiled with mud or smeared with red paint, so that its form is more striking, or by assigning certain comic effects to our images, for that, too, will ensure our remembering them more readily. The things we easily remember when they are real we likewise remember without difficulty when they are figments. But this will be essential—again and again to run over rapidly in the mind all the original places in order to refresh the images.[5]

[5] *Ad Herennium,* III, xxii.

Our author has clearly got hold of the idea of helping memory by arousing emotional affects through these striking and unusual images, beautiful or hideous, comic or obscene. And it is clear that he is thinking of human images, of human figures wearing crowns or purple cloaks, bloodstained or smeared with paint, of human figures dramatically engaged in some activity—doing something. We feel that we have moved into an extraordinary world as we run over his places with the rhetoric student, imagining on the places such very peculiar images. Quintilian's anchor and weapon as memory images, though much less exciting, are easier to understand than the weirdly populated memory to which the author of Ad Herennium introduces us.

It is easy to see why the method of loci helps one to learn the order of events when the path to be followed in looking for the stored items is a logical or familiar one. The principle is similar to that used in rhyming: the external structure of the mnemonic device enforces a unique ordering. But, it is not at all clear why placing objects in imaginary locations should make it any easier to remember the objects themselves. This is exactly the psychological problem raised by the introduction of mnemonics. It is one thing to say that these tricks are simply clever utilizations of well-known psychological processes. It is another thing to illustrate how those psychological processes are actually used. It is interesting to note, however, that the rules of Ad Herennium emphasized a number of techniques well-established by today's experimental psychologists: for one, rehearse (". . . run over rapidly in the mind . . ."), for another, unique and isolated items are remembered best.

ANALYTIC SUBSTITUTIONS

A favorite technique for learning long lists of items or numbers is to change numbers into sounds, sounds into words, and words into sentences. Credit for this system seems to lie with Stanislaus Mink von Wenussheim (otherwise known as Winckelmann) who developed a scheme for representing numbers by consonants in 1648. Winckelmann's scheme evidently is the basis for almost every subsequent memory system, although few people ever gave him credit. One elaboration of this method which gained favor (and also resentment and lawsuits) in London and Washington in the 1890's was that of Loisette.[6]

[6] Although the Encyclopaedia Britannica (see Mitchell, 1910) credits the German Winckelmann with the invention of the number-consonant alphabet in 1648, the idea evidently was first originated in its modern form by the French mathematician Pietro Herigon in 1634. (Personal communication from M. N. Young.) For a comprehensive discussion of the history and techniques of mnemonics see the articles

Loisette proposed three basic ways by which the user of his system might choose to relate arbitrary items to one another:

1. *Inclusion:* Different items may overlap in meaning or ideas or sounds.

2. *Exclusion:* One word may exclude the other or both words may relate to one and the same thing, but occupy opposite positions in regard to it.

3. *Concurrence:* Impressions or ideas may accidentally or casually appear together.

Loisette's system involves forming relations among all the items which are to be learned by various (and sometimes strained) applications of these 3 basic principles.

Numbers are more difficult to learn than words, so Loisette suggests a special technique for them, namely his "own" (slight) modification of the Winckelmann scheme. Here is an excerpt from Loisette. Note that the substitution of numbers to letters is to be used only by those pupils who failed to learn numbers by a more basic application of the three rules of memory.

ANALYTIC SUBSTITUTIONS *

PROFESSOR A. LOISETTE

ANOTHER METHOD FOR REMEMBERING DATES AND FIGURES.

This lesson in figures is given for the benefit of those who have not yet mastered Numeric Thinking. The pupil will appreciate its practical value the moment he masters the key to it.

This is given in the next few pages, and it will be found to be easy of comprehension and interesting to a surprising degree.

(starting with *Mnemotecnia*) in the *Enciclopedia Universal Ilustrada, Europeo-Americana* (Madrid: Espasa-Calpe, S.A. Vol. 35, pp. 1148–1159). Also see *Herigon, Pietro* and *Winkelmann, Johann Justus* in Young (1961).

In the discussions that follow I use excerpts from Loisette to illustrate the number-consonant system primarily because, of the books available to me, his presentation was the most enjoyable.

* A. Loisette. *Assimilative Memory or How to Attend and Never Forget.* New York: Funk and Wagnalls Co. 1896. Pages 66–67 and 74–76.

The whole thing is in a nutshell. Numbers, as such, are abstractions and hard to be remembered. To make them hard to forget, we translate them into words or phrases. These are easily remembered and they always instantly give back the figures they stand for.

We represent the figures 1, 2, 3, 4, 5, 6, 7, 8, 9, and 0, by certain *consonants;* and then, as the vowels [a, e, i, o, u, and y, together with w] have *no numerical* value assigned to them, we turn dates or any numbers into translating *words,* which will always tell us precisely the figures the words stand for.

As this simple process enables us to remember any dates or numbers with *absolute certainty,* the pupil will be pleased to know that he can learn *how it is done* by only *one thoughtful* perusal.

The questions at the bottom of each page constitute an invaluable aid to test the accuracy of his knowledge and the correctness of his inferences.

The nought and the nine digits are *represented* by the following *consonants* when they are *sounded* or *pronounced;* viz., 0 (nought) by s, z, or c^{soft} as in cease, 1 by t, th, or d, 2 by n, 3 by m, 4 by r, 5 by l, 6 by sh, j, ch, or g^{soft} as in the first g of George, 7 g^{hard} as in Gorge, k, c^{hard} as in cane, q, or ng, 8 by f or v, and 9 by b or p.

Ample practice in translating the sounded consonants of words into figures, or of figures into the sounded consonants of words will now be given. If the reader can *remember* the foregoing consonant equivalents of figures in connection with the tabulated Figure Alphabet on page 116, he can at once pass on through the book. If not, he must carefully study the intervening pages with painstaking—for when once learned, no further difficulty can arise.

The tabulated Figure Alphabet of this lesson expresses the consonant values of the nought and nine digits in perpendicular columns, as under nought (0) are placed *s, z,* and c^{soft}; under nine are placed *b* and *p;* under six are placed *sh, j, ch,* and g^{soft}, & c. Only those who possess first-rate natural memories can learn the equivalents of the sounded consonants in figures from this table. But when learned in this way, the pupil requires much practice in translating words into figures and figures into words. Even this exceptional pupil had better carefully study the ensuing examples.

The first thing to be done is to learn *which* consonants are used to stand for and represent the nought (0) and 1, 2, 3, 4, 5, 6, 7, 8 and 9. Let the student re-

1. Is it possible to exaggerate the importance of this lesson? 2. When the pupil appreciate its practical value? 3. Where is this key given? 4. Are numbers hard to remember? 5. How do we make them hard to forget? 6. By what are the figures represented? 7. What letters have no numerical value assigned to them? 8. What do the questions at the bottom of each page constitute?

member that we use vowels to make words with, but we do not give the vowels [a, e, i, o, u], or w, or y, *any number value whatever.*

WE REPRESENT THE NOUGHT OR CYPHER [0] BY THE CONSONANTS S, Z, OR C^{soft} [AS IN *cease*].

The figure value of "sew," therefore equals or is represented by a cipher [0]. S = 0, and the vowel "e" and the consonant "w" have *no figure value.* Cannot the student understand at once that Say = 0, See = 0, Ease = 0, Is = 0, and Zoe = 0, and Seize = 00, Size = 00, Sauce = 00?

The following is another way of fixing in mind this first rule.

If the capital letter S were cut into two parts, and the bottom half attached to the top half, it would make a nought (0). *So it is easy to remember that S represents* 0. C^{soft} as in *cease* has the same sound as S, and should therefore stand for the same figure, *viz.,* 0; and Z is a cognate of S—that is, it is *made by the same organs of speech in the same position* as when making S, only it is an undertone, and S is a whispered letter. Besides Z should represent 0 because it begins the word Zero—C^{soft} should also stand for 0 for the additional reason that C^{soft} begins the word cipher. *In translating a word into figures we always turn S, Z, or C^{soft} into nought (0); in turning figures into words we always translate a nought (0) into S, Z, or C^{soft}.*

1 IS REPRESENTED BY THE CONSONANT "T," "TH," or "D."

Toy = 1. As "t" stands for 1, and o and y are vowels, and have no figure value, the numerical value of Toy *must* be 1.

Thee = 1, *Thou* = 1, *Day* = 1, *Dew* = 1, *This* = 10, *Thus* = 10, *Does* = 10, *Ties* = 10, *Toes* = 10, *Deed* = 11, *Doth* = 11, *To-day* = 11, *Tattoo* = 11, *Tut* = 11, *Toad* = 11, *Tied* = 11, *Sat* = 01, *Said* = 01, *Seat* = 01, *Days* = 10, *Toys* = 10, *These* = 10, *Those* = 10.

"t" stands for 1, because it is made with *one* downward stroke. "h" has no figure value except when it is united with "s" or "c" in sh or ch, and there-fore "th" *must* represent 1, and d, being the cognate of "t," it is represented by 1. Hence we translate "t," "th," and "d" by the figure 1, and when we want to represent 1, by letters, we translate it into t, th, or d.

— — —

For convenience of reference I now give the Figure Alphabet tabulated.

1. In translating a word into figures, what do we always do? 2. By what letters is the figure 1 represented? 3. Why does "t" stand for 1? 4. When does the letter "h" have a figure value? 5. By what is 2 represented? 6. Why? 7. How do we represent 3? 8. Why? 9. By what consonant is 4 represented? 10. Why?

0	1	2	3	4	5	6	7	8	9
S	t	n	m	r	l	sh	g^{hard}	f	b
	th								
						j	k	v	p
Z	d								
							c^{hard}		
						ch			
C^{soft}							q		
						g^{soft}			
							ng		

If the pupil has mastered the Figure Alphabet he will proceed with the greatest satisfaction and profit. If he has not mastered it, let him carefully review the foregoing pages of this chapter, and then he can advance with the assurance of meeting no difficulties.

HOW TO FIND WORDS WITH WHICH TO TRANSLATE DATES AND NUMBERS.

It is a simple and easy process; knowing exactly what consonants are used to represent each of the numbers, you simply write at the side of the numbers to be turned into words the consonants which stand for them; and using any vowels you please, you find out by experimenting what words can translate the figures. Suppose you wish to find out what words will translate the date of the settlement of Jamestown, Va., 1607. You place the figures under each other as below, and then you place at the right hand of each figure the consonants which translate it.

1 = t, th, d.
6 = sh, j, ch, g soft (as in gem).
0 = s, z, c soft (as in cease).
7 = g hard, k, c hard, q, and ng.

By experimenting you soon find the following phrases will represent 1607; as, "A Dutch Song," "Dash a Sack," "To wash a Sock," "The Choosing," "The Chasing," "Touches a Key," &c.

Try the date of the adoption of the Constitution of the United States, 1787. Writing down the numbers as before, you place t, th, d, opposite 1; g hard, k, c hard, q, ng, opposite 7; f and v, opposite 8; g hard, k, c hard, q, and ng, opposite 7; and then you soon find translating words, as follows: "To give a Key," "The giving," "The quaffing," "The Coughing," &c.

In all cases you must carefully comply with the rules and explanations heretofore given. A little practice will enable you to dispense with writing down the figures and the consonants which represent them; but at first pains must be taken in the above way to secure accuracy.

Try 1636, the date of the founding of Harvard College: You obtain "Dash a midge," "The chum age," "Teach much," "To show my joy," &c.

The founding of Yale College in 1701 gives: "Took a seat," "The cost," "The quest," "The cast," "A tax due," or "Took a city," &c.

Sometimes the first consonants only of words are used. Comenius, Educational Reformer (things before words, pictured illustrations, &c.) and Moravian Bishop, was born 1592: or (1) Things (5) Well (9) Pictured (2) Now. He died 1671; or A (1) Teaching (6) Churchman (7) Gave (1) Out.

Loisette goes on and on, but the technique is clear. Obviously, for all the complicated rules, Loisette's (or, more properly, Winckelmann's) scheme is identical in principle to the "one is a bun, two is a shoe, . . ." scheme illustrated by Miller, Galanter, and Pribram. These systems do seem to work, although at the cost of a large initial investment by the user in the time and effort required to learn the system in the first place. For example, the author of a recent book *How to Improve Your Memory* says this about the number-consonant system: [7]

If you learn the system and practice it constantly, you acquire facility in translation and in interpreting your translations. You might decide whether you consider the system worth learning and using by selecting a few numbers that you wish to remember—such as your social security number, the number of your bank account, and a telephone number or two—and (1) seeing whether you can translate them into words or phrases, then (2) deciding whether you could remember the translations more easily than the numbers.

As for appointments, it would probably be better to enter your appointment for April 16 at 4:00 on your calendar than to keep it on your mind to "ride ashore."

[7] James W. Weinland. *How to Improve Your Memory*. New York: Barnes and Noble, 1957. Copyright 1957 by Barnes and Noble, Inc. With permission of publisher.

1. What would be your method of procedure? 2. What must be done in all cases? 3. What will a little practice enable you to do? 4. What must be done to secure accuracy at first? 5. Deal with an original date in the way indicated here. 6. In dealing with the date of the foundation of Yale College, would the phrase "taxes due" express 1701? 7. If not, why? 8. Can you translate into a word or phrase the date of your own birth? 9. Translate into words or phrases the birth and death dates of some of the historic characters which you admire most. 10. Keep a record of these words or phrases for future examination.

The translation device is useful for the performance of memory stunts with numbers. But the average person will probably consider it more of a curiosity than a helpful device.

This particular book, by James D. Weinland, a retired Professor of Business Psychology, describes the principles of most mnemonic systems without dogmatism and with an attempt to connect each method with the findings of experimental psychology. More important, Weinland provides us with statements about the limitations of each technique, something seldom found in popular writing.

What is it about mnemonic systems that improves our ability to memorize? All the systems seem to share common emphasis on organization. Evidently one just cannot go about memorizing things as they happen. One has to organize the material, group it into meaningful structures, form unique and bizarre associations, and tuck it away in memory according to a formal, orderly plan. If the material does not lend itself to visualization and associations as it stands, it must be transformed by the use of key words or analytic substitutions until images can be used.

The emphasis on the structure of stored material, whether it be imposed by rhythmic techniques, formally learned memory loci, or unique vivid imagery, indicates that the difficulty in memorizing material has more to do with retrieval than with storage itself. If storage of information were the bottleneck, one would hardly wish to use a mnemonic device which increased the amount of information to be stored. Yet every technique we have examined appears to do just that. Nowhere in the literature can we find a system which tries to condense and simplify the material: every system enriches and adds to the information. The implication is that organization plays an important role in retrieval. Why should this be?

ORGANIZATION AND MEMORY

The retrieval of material from a large capacity system such as our long-term or secondary memory must be quite a different process from that of retrieval from a small capacity storage system, such as primary memory. With any large memory, a random search of the contents becomes impractical. In fact, the knowledge that the information which is sought is stored in the memory is, by itself, useless. The necessity of an organizational scheme is easily illustrated by the problem faced by a large library. If a book is misplaced on the library shelves, it might as well be lost. It does not matter at all that the book is actually within the library; if it is not in its proper place, it will not be found by any ordinary search. So it is with human memory: even if the information of interest is there, it is useless unless it can be reached. How do we search our memory for a fact which we know is there? The problem is to get to the proper associates of the target; once there, the rest flows naturally.

When we deal with verbal material, associations are readily available through the semantic structure of the items. We have already read, however, that our ability to learn verbal material after one presentation seems to be limited to a few words by the principles of the magical number 7. Is it possible to organize verbal material in such a way as to overcome this limitation?

A number of recent studies of memory have emphasized the role of organization in the learning of verbal material. These studies appear to provide us with a link between the limitations of primary memory and the large capacity of secondary memory through the mechanism of proper and efficient organization. The basic idea arises from Miller's realization that although we seem able to learn no more than seven (plus or minus two) things at any one time, each of these things can be rich in structure and meaning.

A rather general principle seems to be emerging: people group and categorize the objects they intend to learn. When we look for evidence of this principle, we find it everywhere. Telephone numbers are subdivided into smaller sequences. The names of the months are divided into the four seasons. Poetry is easier to learn than prose. Children naturally form sing-song rhythms of lists they wish to remember. For example, consider how the alphabet is learned. To a child the alphabet is a long, rather arbitrary, string of items. Children go through seemingly endless hours of recitation while they get all the letters together, but they do it in a nice, orderly fashion. They use a rhyme which divides the 26 letters into 3 chunks, each chunk having 2 elements, each element having 2 units, and each unit having 1 to 4 letters. Thus: [(ab—cd) (ef—g)] [(hi—jk) (lmno—p)] [(qrs—tuv) (w—xyz)]. What better example of all the principles we have just enumerated: there is rhythm; there is rhyme; no single chunk is large enough to strain the capacity of primary memory. Do you doubt that you learned the alphabet in this way; do you claim that you know the letters as one whole, smoothly organized unit? Then say the alphabet backwards and see if the places you stumble don't match up with the boundaries between the groups you once used.

Grouping, categorization, clustering: these principles are even showing up in one of the least likely places, the experimental laboratory. Slowly there is realization that experimental subjects form groups of the items they are trying to learn. Bousfield (1953), Bousfield and Cohen (1955), and Bousfield and Sedgewick (1944), noted clustering of words in the words recalled by their subjects. Tulving (1962, 1964) has examined the response strategies used by subjects who learn lists of unrelated words. He finds that subjects organize the words and that once formed, these organizations tend to stick throughout the rest of the experiment. That is, once a subject puts together some of the words on the list he is trying to learn, he tends always to recall them together, regardless of the way that the words are scrambled up by the experimenter. Moreover, learning of new words builds on the previously acquired structures.

The general conclusion that seems inescapable is that material is not easily learned unless it has some structure. If the structure is not already present, it has to be provided, either by the categorization performed by the subject or by application of a formal system of mnemonic rules. Moreover, the structure of organization used in the secondary memory seems to be determined by the limitations of primary memory. These principles seem obvious, yet they play little part in the theories of most psychologists. Organizational factors are passed off rather quickly in most discussions of memory. One of the exceptions seems to be the recent papers of George Mandler (1967a, 1967b) on organization and memory. Mandler has examined directly the categorizations used by subjects and finds that he can manipulate the amount of material remembered by manipulations on the organizational structure of the material. He summarizes his basic theoretical viewpoint in this way:

When a subject is required to memorize relatively large sets of words, the mechanism apparently involves two separate processes: short-term, or primary memory, which produces recall of the words immediately following the output; and organized memory, which typically includes earlier words from the list.

— — —

Since the present concern is not with short-term or immediate memory in the sense of recovering items from some temporary or buffer storage, it seems likely that the value of items to be recalled per chunk is below seven; for working purposes, and in light of some of our subsequent data, a value of 5 ± 2 seems more appropriate.

To recapitulate: given a set of words, a human organism categorizes them and, if the length of the list requires an extended organization, arranges the categories in turn into superordinate categories (Mandler, 1967a, pp. 332–333. Copyright 1967 by Academic Press. With permission.).

When we apply these comments to the readings on memory systems, we see that the power of mnemonic systems may be the result of a very simple principle: they reduce long, unrelated strings of material into short, related lists. Mnemonic systems provide us with the rules and techniques for shortening the sequence that is to be learned and finding meaning, even where there appears to be none.

A common objection to mnemonic systems is that they increase the amount of material that is to be learned. This is certainly true, in a limited sense. All systems make the user learn rhymes or associations or images in addition to the basic material that he is really interested in retaining, but these additions may actually amount to a decrease in the amount of actual material which must be learned. The span of human memory is limited by the number of meaningful items presented to it, not by physical variables such as the number of words or images. Thus, a mnemonic technique may actually decrease the number of meaningful units in the material which is to be learned. Formally, a sequence of four digits is shorter than an image of those four digits arranged in a meaningful pattern. But when we try to learn the digits, we need to learn four things; when we try to learn the image, only one thing need be learned, the pattern.

We can illustrate the points by looking at specific examples provided by our readings. The key word system, illustrated by the transformation rule that "one is a bun, two is a shoe, . . ." is a good example of a technique that can only lengthen the sequence to be remembered. The rule transforms sequences of digits into sequences of words, but with an exact one-to-one equivalence of one for the other. Thus, any improvement in memory performance that results from this rule must come about from the added meaning that the words provide, not from a reduction in the number of items to be learned.

The number-consonant system (of Winckelmann, illustrated by the excerpt from Loisette) is a more powerful mnemonic device than the key word system because it manages both to add meaning to a sequence of digits and simultaneously to shorten the actual number of items which need be learned. For example, in his paper on the magical number 7 (Chapter 5), Miller discussed an experiment by Sidney Smith on a method of encoding a string of items into a shorter string. Smith had his subjects learn sequences of binary numbers by encoding each group of three binary digits into one octal number. In this way they could almost triple the number of binary digits they could retain. The number-consonant scheme uses a similar principle to reduce the number of elements which must be retained, but then goes one important step further: it adds meaning to the string.

Consider how one would go about learning the sequence of binary digits: 001100001001100001101010001111111100000. This is more than our memory span can encompass. We can use Smith's trick and encode them into octal digits: 1411415217740 (see page 77). This is a much shorter sequence, but it is still too long to be learned easily. But now, if we apply the number-consonant transformation, we get *trttrtlntkkrs*. After a moment's thought we realize that we can change those letters into the equivalent sequence of *trd drt ln tng grs*. This consonant sequence leads us to the word-picture of a *tired dirty lion eating grass*. Thus, we have reduced 39 binary numbers to 13 octal ones, 13 octal numbers to 5 words, and finally, 5 words to one picture. This mnemonic system is powerful (for the practiced user) because it tremendously reduces the amount of material we need to learn. The system costs effort, however, first in the hours of practice it takes to learn the rules, and then in the effort it takes to apply them. This example of mnemonic techniques somewhat destroys their charm, but it should also illustrate their power.

Summing up, it appears that the organization important for efficient learning is of two forms. One corresponds to the organization that is used in human storage itself. The other corresponds to the organization of the material which is to be learned: chunking and categorization. If we had to state rules for efficient memorization, they might look something like these:

1. *Small basic units:* The material to be learned must be divisible into small, self-contained sections, with no more than four or five individual items in any section.

2. *Internal organization:* The sections must be organized so that the various parts fit together in a logical, self-ordering structure.

3. *External organization:* Some relationship must be established between the material to be learned and material which has already been learned, so that one fits neatly within the other.

The various memory systems which we have examined provide systematic techniques for taking arbitrary material and forming it into organizations which obey these three rules. The known properties of human memory suggest reasons for these principles. To summarize these reasons briefly, the requirement that material be categorized into small groups seems to result from the limited capacity of primary memory. The requirement for a logical ordering of sections (categories or chunks) is imposed by the extreme difficulty of learning order relationships. The requirement for rich associations to previously learned material seems to be a requirement of the retrieval process, for the well-learned associations provide the starting place for the search of memory when recall is desired.

We are now able to create a general maxim for those who wish to improve their memory. If you wish to learn something, rather than plunge blindly ahead reciting the material endlessly, it would be best to first summarize briefly its overall meaning and structure, second, to decide how it relates to what you already know and, finally, to divide the material into a small set of logical subdivisions.

By following these procedures, one automatically uses a number of psychological principles known to improve learning. The procedure forces full attention to be applied to the material; it forces partial learning of the whole and partial learning by parts; it provides components of sufficiently small size to be learned as one "chunk"; and it provides structure, both to relate the individual chunks to one another and to integrate the whole with what has been learned previously.

The study of memory systems have offered us something new, if only because in the past 2000 years they have emphasized principles that are only now being studied. Whether mnemonic techniques use principles which differ from those already known to us in more fundamental ways than suggested here cannot be said until we study them in the controlled environment of the laboratory.

SUGGESTED READINGS

On the workings of mnemonics, little new is being said at the present time, although the first faint signs of research are being noted. The revival can be traced to the influence of the book *Plans and the Structure of Behavior* by Miller, Galanter and Pribram, so the interested reader should certainly start there. Chapter 10 is the most relevant, but most of the book will be of general interest. At the present time, the few published studies on mnemonics are little more than demonstrations of their effects (and failures), but that is the way it must be until enough concrete facts are gathered together to enable us to determine the underlying structures.

The organization of memory probably plays the determining role in the importance of mnemonic techniques. Organization is required for retrieval, and unless newly learned material is properly integrated with the old, it may never be recovered from memory. Thus, studies of the organizational properties of memory should lead to the most important breakthroughs in our understanding. These studies need not be restricted to humans: if we learn the general principles underlying the use of any large scale memory they will be applicable to both human and machine systems. For a discussion of some of the literature on large scale memory systems (so called information systems and data management systems) see the last part of Chapter 8, pages 161–176 (and the suggested readings following that chapter).

A fair number of studies on organization of human memory have been performed, many of which are discussed in articles by Mandler (1967a and b). Mandler's articles ought to be read not only for their contents, but also because the references contained there will lead the reader to the rest of the literature. Particularly relevant are papers by Bousfield and Sedgewick (1944), Bousfield (1953), Cofer (1965), Cohen (1963), Katona (1940), and the papers of Tulving (1962, 1964) and Tulving and Pearlstone (1966).

Tulving has argued that the key to memory is retrieval, and the key to retrieval is accessibility. Furthermore, Tulving argues that there is no distinction between primary and secondary memory other than that of accessibility; items which have just been presented have a readily available cue for retrieval, namely, the fact that of all the material stored in memory they occurred last in time. Obviously this cue works only for the very last few items. Tulving has suggested that when we proponents of a separate short-term memory study the loss of newly acquired information, we are really studying the loss of accessibility to that item, most especially the loss of the relevance of the cue "most recently presented items."

Two standard texts which provide extensive summaries of the literature and references are McGeoch and Irion (1952), and Woodworth and Schlosberg (1958, especially pages 743–746).

The journals relevant to the study of mnemonics and organization are the same set listed for Chapter 5, therefore their names are not repeated here.

7

What Is Stored?

Up to this point we have read and discussed a variety of phenomena and mechanisms associated with attention and memory. But we have avoided one basic issue: just what is stored? Unfortunately there are no answers. Some permanent change must occur in the nervous system to maintain information in secondary storage, but whether the change comes about through the addition of new physical links between nerves, through chemical alteration of molecular structure, by changes in threshold levels at nerve junctions, or by some other mechanism, it still remains an unknown, though hotly debated issue. Indeed, it is not even known where information is encoded within the nervous system; is the memory for a specific event at one specific neurological site or is it spread about as some configuration of nervous activity? These basic issues are far from their eventual resolutions.

THE STUDY OF ERRORS

Even if we cannot say much about the physiological representation of the memory trace, we are able to deduce the logical properties of stored material. To do this, we need to rephrase our questions. We can speculate on the logical organization of storage, for some of the properties of stored material can be deduced independently of the particular physiological mechanisms which might be involved. Perhaps the most powerful way to begin is to look at the types of errors that are made when information is retrieved from memory. We assume that an error occurs when only part of the stored representation of an item has been recovered, either because the remainder of the trace has temporarily eluded our attempts to recover it or because it has been lost from the storage. The part that can be recovered tells us something about the organization of the memory. We can examine the relationship of the recovered material to the original: what physical features are still retained; what psychological features; what distortions occur?

In this chapter we examine representative examples of the interpretations drawn from this type of analysis, thereby hoping to describe and illustrate its application and appropriativeness more than to present a complete answer to the main question of this chapter. We will not be without some results, however. We proceed in almost inverse chronological order of the research, starting with short-term memory for simple objects, proceeding to long-term memory for single words, and concluding with long-term memory for events.

ACOUSTIC CONFUSIONS

A simple question, related to the studies of pattern recognition reviewed in Chapter 3, concerns the manner by which simple objects are represented in storage. For example, in what form do we encode letters of the alphabet? If letters were stored in a form analogous to their visual appearance, then we might suspect that as the memory trace became less distinct, letters which were similar in shape (such as P and F) might get confused with one another.

In the 1960's, R. Conrad, at the Applied Psychology Research Unit in Cambridge, England, performed a number of experiments to examine the types of errors subjects make in short-term memory task using visually presented letters as the items to be remembered (Conrad, 1959, 1962, 1964; Conrad and Hull, 1964). Conrad had to perform several experiments. First, he had to show that the errors observed in his experiments were introduced by the memory rather than the perceptual system. Second, he had to determine the nature of confusions caused by deficits in memory. Third, he had to discover the scheme of storage which would lead to the errors which were found.

Conrad was able to demonstrate that items recalled incorrectly were acoustically related to the original items, even when the material had been presented visually. Thus, the stored representation was related to the spoken representation. It is as if rehearsal of verbal material were an auditory (or spoken) process, with the memory being for what has been rehearsed rather than for what has actually been presented. Conrad's results have played an important role in the development of theories of memory, as we have seen in earlier chapters and will see again in the next chapter.

The procedures followed in these experiments are fairly straightforward, but the interpretation of the results is not so simple. The basic datum is the matrix of confusions: the table that indicates the relative frequency with which each possible letter has been confused with each of the other possible letters. If storage were related to the visual form of letters, we would expect that the letter "E" might sometimes be remembered as an "F" and the letter "C" might be remembered as an "S." In fact, we often remember an "E" as a "C" and an "F" as an "S." Although it is very easy to distinguish the matrix resulting from confusions among acoustical representations of letters from that resulting from visual representations, other distinctions are not so easily determined. For example, is the stored representation of letters more closely related to the actual sounds of the spoken letters—an auditory representation—or to the movements or motor commands used to speak the sounds—an articulatory representation? The difference between articulatory and auditory representation is very important in the assessment of theories of speech perception. In order to distinguish among these representations we would need to generate classes of items which differ from one another in one aspect, say articulation, but do not differ much by another aspect, say in their sounds.[1]

Although subtle distinctions are difficult to make from an analysis of confusion in memory, nonetheless, the method promises to be very powerful in determining many of the characteristics of stored material. Recently, this approach has been used to study the linguistic constituents of spoken sounds (Wickelgren, 1965a, 1966a), to determine how a series of items are stored and linked to one another (Conrad, 1965; Wickelgren, 1965b, 1966a, b, c) and to distinguish the properties of short- and long-term storage (Baddeley, 1966).

The form of errors is one way to distinguish short-term memory from longer-term memory. Conrad's results were based on immediate tests of the material. Hence, the acoustic confusions result from short-term or primary memory. In later experiments (for example, Baddeley, 1966), it has been shown that long-term memory is affected by semantic similarity of the learned items but not by acoustic similarity. Thus, it appears that

[1] Throughout this book the terms *acoustical* and *auditory* are used somewhat interchangeably with reference to the encoding of information in memory. This should be interpreted to mean that the encoding is related to some aspect of speech, but no implication should be drawn about the relative importance of either the speech sounds or the speech articulation in the memory encoding.

the acoustical coding is a temporary phenomenon, restricted to primary memory. Evidently material stored in long-term memory has had a more thorough analysis so that semantics take precedence over acoustics.

To summarize briefly: when we hear or see a word, the physical form must be transduced into a physiological representation and then decoded into its meaningful components. Conrad's experiments imply that during the process of decoding the incoming item, we store it temporarily in auditory form. Early in the process we must have some image of the actual physical word, be it initially visual or auditory. Later, in primary memory, it gets transformed to an auditory form, then still later, in secondary memory, the meaning gets established, probably with the aid of context: the material which preceded and followed it.

THE TIP OF THE TONGUE PROBLEM

What happens when we go in the reverse direction, generating a word to be spoken or written? In this case we start with the meaning or the context and then try to find the word in secondary memory. Most of the time this process occurs rapidly and automatically. We speak and write spontaneously, with little awareness of how each individual word has been retrieved. Sometimes, however, we fall into difficulties, annoying to the person who suffers them, but of great value in our attempt to understand how individual words are stored. One particularly tantalizing phenomenon, especially rich in the insight it gives into the working of retrieval from secondary storage, occurs when we get into a state of partial knowledge about a word. In this particular state, we search for a particular word in memory. Yet, even though we are certain that we know the item which we seek, we cannot quite snatch it into consciousness; we say that the word is "on the tip of the tongue."

The aspect of the tip of the tongue state that most frustrates those who experience it is the extremely long duration that it may last. It is just this point, however, that makes the state valuable to the experimental psychologist: there is time to find out what is happening. Two psychologists at Harvard University, Roger Brown and David McNeill, have used the results of their studies of the tip of the tongue state to speculate on the organization of human memory. In order to do their studies Brown and McNeill first had to devise an experimental technique for inducing the tip of the tongue state in their laboratory subjects. Then they had to develop a procedure for probing the subjects to see how much was really known about the words which the subjects claimed to have found in their memories, yet were unable to extract. Brown and McNeill describe their study in this way.

THE "TIP OF THE TONGUE" PHENOMENON *

ROGER BROWN and DAVID MC NEILL

William James wrote, in 1890: "Suppose we try to recall a forgotten name. The state of our consciousness is peculiar. There is a gap therein; but no mere gap. It is a gap that is intensely active. A sort of wraith of the name is in it, beckoning us in a given direction, making us at moments tingle with the sense of our closeness and then letting us sink back without the longed-for term. If wrong names are proposed to us, this singularly definite gap acts immediately so as to negate them. They do not fit into its mould. And the gap of one word does not feel like the gap of another, all empty of content as both might seem necessarily to be when described as gaps."

The "tip of the tongue" (TOT) state involves a failure to recall a word of which one has knowledge. The evidence of knowledge is either an eventually successful recall or else an act of recognition that occurs, without additional training, when recall has failed. The class of cases defined by the conjunction of knowledge and a failure of recall is a large one. The TOT state, which James described, seems to be a small subclass in which recall is felt to be imminent.

For several months we watched for TOT states in ourselves. Unable to recall the name of the street on which a relative lives, one of us thought of *Congress* and *Corinth* and *Concord* and then looked up the address and learned that it was *Cornish*. The words that had come to mind have certain properties in common with the word that had been sought (the "target word"); all four begin with *Co;* all are two-syllable words; all put the primary stress on the first syllable. After this experience we began putting direct questions to ourselves when we fell into the TOT state, questions as to the number of syllables in the target word, its initial letter, etc.

Brown and McNeill devised an experimental technique for inducing the TOT state in their subjects. The procedure was simple: subjects were

* Roger Brown and David McNeill. The "tip of the tongue" phenomenon. *J. Verb. Learn. Verb. Behav.*, 1966, 5, 325–337. Copyright 1966 by Academic Press. With permission of authors and publisher.

presented with the definition of an uncommon English word and were asked to supply the word. In a preliminary experiment on nine subjects, the procedure appeared to be successful. To quote Brown and McNeill:

> In 57 instances an S [subject] was, in fact, "seized" by a TOT state. The signs of it were unmistakable; he would appear to be in a mild torment, something like the brink of a sneeze, and if he found the word his relief was considerable. While searching for the target S told us all the words that came to his mind. He volunteered the information that some of them resembled the target in sound but not in meaning; others he was sure were similar in meaning, but not in sound. The E [experimenter] intruded on S's agony with two questions: (a) How many syllables has the target word? (b) What is its first letter? Answers to the first question were correct in 47 percent of all cases and answers to the second were correct in 51 percent of the cases.

The procedure was refined by eliciting more information from the subjects about the exact state of their knowledge of the target word while in the TOT state. In a test of 56 subjects, the experimental procedure was able to yield 360 instances of a TOT state. Of this total, 233 of the instances yielded usable data. Brown and McNeill analyzed their data for the types of partial information that their subjects were able to give: number of syllables, initial letter, syllabic stress, letters in various positions, suffixes, and other aspects.

The preliminary characterization of the data was that "when complete recall of a word is not presently possible but is felt to be imminent, one can often correctly recall the general type of the word; *generic* recall may succeed when particular recall fails." After the complete analysis of the data had been completed, Brown and McNeill were able to develop this survey of their experimental and theoretical conclusions.[2]

Conclusions

When complete recall of a word has not occurred but is felt to be imminent there is likely to be accurate generic recall. Generic recall of the *abstract form* variety is evidenced by S's knowledge of the number of syllables in the target and of the location of the primary stress. Generic recall of the *partial* variety is evidenced by S's knowledge of letters in the target word. This knowledge shows a bowed serial-position effect since it is better for the ends of a word than for the middle and somewhat better for beginning positions than for final positions. The accuracy of generic recall is greater when S is near the target (complete recall is imminent) than when S is far from the target. A person experiencing generic recall is able to judge the relative similarity to the

[2] R. Brown and D. McNeill. *Op. cit.* Pages 333–336.

target of words that occur to him and these judgments are based on the features of words that figure in partial and abstract form recall.

DISCUSSION

The facts of generic recall are relevant to theories of speech perception, reading, the understanding of sentences, and the organization of memory. We have not worked out all the implications. In this section we first attempt a model of the TOT process and then try to account for the existence of generic memory.

A Model of the Process

Let us suppose (with Katz and Fodor, 1963, and many others) that our long-term memory for words and definitions is organized into the functional equivalent of a dictionary. In real dictionaries, those that are books, entries are ordered alphabetically and bound in place. Such an arrangement is too simple and too inflexible to serve as a model for a mental dictionary. We will suppose that words are entered on keysort cards instead of pages and that the cards are punched for various features of the words entered. With real cards, paper ones, it is possible to retrieve from the total deck any subset punched for a common feature by putting a metal rod through the proper hole. We will suppose that there is in the mind some speedier equivalent of this retrieval technique.

The model will be described in terms of a single example. When the target word was *sextant,* Ss heard the definition: "A navigational instrument used in measuring angular distances, especially the altitude of sun, moon, and stars at sea." This definition precipitated a TOT state in 9 Ss of the total 56. The [similar meaning] (SM) words included: *astrolabe, compass, dividers,* and *protractor.* The [similar sound] (SS) words included: *secant, sextet,* and *sexton.*

The problem begins with a definition rather than a word and so S must enter his dictionary backwards, or in a way that would be backwards and quite impossible for the dictionary that is a book. It is not impossible with keysort cards, providing we suppose that the cards are punched for some set of semantic features. Perhaps these are the semantic "markers" that Katz and Fodor (1963) postulate in their account of the comprehension of sentences. We will imagine that it is somehow possible to extract from the definition a set of markers and that these are, in the present case: "navigation, instrument, having to do with geometry." Metal rods thrust into the holes for each of these features might fish up such a collection of entries as: *astrolabe, compass, dividers,* and *protractor.* This first retrieval, which is in response to the definition, must be semantically based and it will not, therefore, account for the appearance of such SS words as *sextet* and *sexton*.

There are four major kinds of outcome of the first retrieval and these outcomes correspond with the four main things that happen to Ss in the TOT experiment. We will assume that a definition of each word retrieved is entered on its card and that it is possible to check the input definition against those on the cards. The first possible outcome is that *sextant* is retrieved along with *compass* and *astrolabe* and the others and that the definitions are specific enough so that the one entered for *sextant* registers as matching the input and all the others as not-matching. This is the case of correct recall; S has found a word that matches the definition and it is the intended word. The second possibility is that *sextant* is not among the words retrieved and, in addition, the definitions entered for those retrieved are so imprecise that one of them (the definition for *compass,* for example) registers as matching the input. In this case S thinks he has found the target though he really has not. The third possibility is that *sextant* is not among the words retrieved, but the definitions entered for those retrieved are specific enough so that none of them will register a match with the input. In this case, S does not know the word and realizes the fact. The above three outcomes are the common ones and none of them represents a TOT state.

In the TOT case the first retrieval must include a card with the definition of *sextant* entered on it but with the word itself incompletely entered. The card might, for instance, have the following information about the word: two-syllables, initial s, final t. The entry would be a punchcard equivalent of S___ ___T. Perhaps an incomplete entry of this sort is James's "singularly definite gap" and the basis for generic recall.

The S with a correct definition, matching the input, and an incomplete word entry will know that he knows the word, will feel that he almost has it, that it is on the tip of his tongue. If he is asked to guess the number of syllables and the initial letter he should, in the case we have imagined, be able to do so. He should also be able to produce SS words. The features that appear in the incomplete entry (two-syllables, initial s, and final t) can be used as the basis for a second retrieval. The subset of cards defined by the intersection of all three features would include cards for *secant* and *sextet.* If one feature were not used then *sexton* would be added to the set.

Which of the facts about the TOT state can now be accounted for? We know that Ss were able, when they had not recalled a target, to distinguish between words resembling the target in sound (SS words) and words resembling the target in meaning only (SM words). The basis for this distinction in the model would seem to be the distinction between the first and second retrievals. Membership in the first subset retrieved defines SM words and membership in the second subset defines SS words.

We know that when S had produced several SS words but had not re-called the target he could sometimes accurately rank-order the SS words for similarity to the target. The model offers an account of this ranking perform-ance. If the incomplete entry for *sextant* includes three features of the word then SS words having only one or two of these features (e.g., *sexton*) should be judged less similar to the target than SS words having all three of them (e.g., *secant*).

When an SS word has all of the features of the incomplete entry (as do *secant* and *sextet* in our example) what prevents its being mistaken for the target? Why did not the S who produced *sextet* think that the word was "right?" Because of the definitions. The forms meet all the requirements of the incomplete entry but the definitions do not match.

The TOT state often ended in recognition; i.e., S failed to recall the word but when E read out *sextant* S recognized it as the word he had been seek-ing. The model accounts for this outcome as follows. Suppose that there is only the incomplete entry S___ ___T in memory, plus the definition. The E now says (in effect) that there exists a word *sextant* which has the definition in question. The word *sextant* then satisfies all the data points available to S; it has the right number of syllables, the right initial letter, the right final letter, and it is said to have the right definition. The result is recognition.

The proposed account has some testable implications. Suppose that E were to read out, when recall failed, not the correct word *sextant* but an invented word like *sekrant* or *saktint* which satisfies the incomplete entry as well as does *sextant* itself. If S had nothing but the incomplete entry and E's testimony to guide him then he should "recognize" the invented words just as he recognizes *sextant*.

The account we have given does not accord with intuition. Our intuitive notion of recognition is that the features which could not be called were actually in storage but less accessible than the features that were recalled. To stay with our example, intuition suggests that the features of *sextant* that could not be recalled, the letters between the first and the last, were entered on the card but were less "legible" than the recalled features. We might imagine them printed in small letters and faintly. When, however, the E reads out the word *sextant,* then S can make out the less legible parts of his entry and, since the total entry matches E's word, S recognizes it. This sort of recognition should be "tighter" than the one described previously. *Sekrant* and *saktint* would be rejected.

We did not try the effect of invented words and we do not know how they would have been received but among the outcomes of the actual experiment there is one that strongly favors the faint-entry theory. Subjects in a TOT state, after all, sometimes recalled the target word without any prompting. The in-complete entry theory does not admit of such a possibility. If we suppose that the entry is not S___ ___T but something more like Sex *tan*T (with the italicized lower-case letters representing the faint-entry section) we must still explain how it happens that the faintly entered, and at first inaccessible, middle letters are made accessible in the case of recall.

Perhaps it works something like this. The features that are first recalled operate as we have suggested, to retrieve a set of SS words. Whenever an SS word (such as *secant*) includes middle letters that are matched in the faintly entered section of the target then those faintly entered letters become accessible. The match brings out the missing parts the way heat brings out anything written in lemon juice. In other words, when *secant* is retrieved the target entry grows from Sex *tan*T to SEx *t*ANT. The retrieval of *sextet* brings out the remaining letters and S recalls the complete word—*sextant*.

It is now possible to explain the one as yet unexplained outcome of the TOT experiment. Subjects whose state ended in recall had, before they found the target, more correct information about it than did Ss whose state ended in recognition. More correct information means fewer features to be brought out by duplication in SS words and so should mean a greater likelihood that all essential features will be brought out in a short period of time.

All of the above assumes that each word is entered in memory just once, on a single card. There is another possibility. Suppose that there are entries for *sextant* on several different cards. They might all be incomplete, but at different points, or, some might be incomplete and one or more of them complete. The several cards would be punched for different semantic markers and perhaps for different associations so that the entry recovered would vary with the rule of retrieval. With this conception we do not require the notion of faint entry. The difference between features commonly recalled, such as the first and last letters, and features that are recalled with difficulty or perhaps only recognized, can be rendered in another way. The more accessible features are entered on more cards or else the cards on which they appear are punched for more markers; in effect, they are wired into a more extended associative net.

The Reason for Generic Recall

In adult minds words are stored in both visual and auditory terms and between the two there are complicated rules of translation. Generic recall involves letters (or phonemes), affixes, syllables, and stress location. In this section we will discuss only letters (legible forms) and will attempt to explain a single effect—the serial position effect in the recall of letters. It is not clear how far the explanation can be extended.

In brief overview this is the argument. The design of the English language is such that one word is usually distinguished from all others in a more-than-minimal way, i.e., by more than a single letter in a single position. It is consequently *possible* to recognize words when one has not stored the complete letter sequence. The evidence is that we do not store the complete sequence if we do not have to. We begin by attending chiefly to initial and final letters and storing these. The order of attention and of storage favors the ends of words because the ends carry more information than the middles. An incomplete entry will serve for recognition, but if words are to be produced (or recalled) they must be stored in full. For most words, then, it is eventually necessary to attend to the middle letters. Since end letters have been attended to from the first they should always be more clearly entered or more elaborately connected than middle letters. When recall is required, of words that are not very familiar to S, as it was in our experiment, the end letters should often be accessible when the middle are not.

In building pronounceable sequences the English language, like all other languages, utilizes only a small fraction of its combinatorial possibilities. If a language used all possible sequences of phonemes (or letters) its words could be shorter, but they would be much more vulnerable to misconstruction. A change of any single letter would result in reception of a different word. As matters are actually arranged, most changes result in no word at all; for example: *textant, sixtant, sektant.* Our words are highly redundant and fairly indestructible.

The model of memory described by Brown and McNeill assumes that words are stored at specific locations in memory. At each location there are special "markers" which specify the semantic content and associations of the words. In their model, Brown and McNeill suggest that the information necessary to translate from the acoustical representation of each word to the semantic representation is also contained at each storage location. It takes less information about a word to interpret it than it does to generate it, primarily because the interpretation process requires only sufficient information about the word to distinguish it from all other possibilities. Any lack of information about the middle of a word does not necessarily harm the understanding of spoken words. The generation process, on the other hand, requires a complete specification of the entire word, otherwise we would have to speak some words by pronouncing the beginning and ending and mumbling the middle.

It is interesting that Brown and McNeill found no information about the visual properties of words in the TOT state. This might be an artifact of their testing procedure, but more likely it results from the nature of the memory system itself. Certainly we can interpret the results of Conrad's experiments to indicate that words normally are represented in storage auditorally, rather than visually. In this sense, then, the results from the tip of the tongue studies are completely consistent with all the other studies we have examined. Somewhere, however, there must exist visual representations of words, for otherwise we would not be able to read and write them. Moreover, the visual representation must exist in secondary memory and must be used by whatever mechanism translates visual images to auditory images, presumably in the transference of words from visual information storage into primary memory. Of course, it is not necessary to store visual images for all words. We need only store the rules which tell us how to convert one form to the other. In view of the complexity of orthography, however—the rules contain large numbers of exceptions and special cases—it seems more likely that some spelling and pronunciation rules are stored for each word. In any event, it is obvious that someplace we have stored rules or images for visual translation of words, yet we have almost no evidence about them. So far, our results have been restricted to auditory phenomena.

REMEMBERING OR RECONSTRUCTING

We now turn to a more complex subject: the storage for complex events. The next study, our last, should possibly have come first, for it introduces the techniques of inferring the properties of memory from the types of errors made by subjects. The investigations were performed in Cambridge, England in the 1920's and 30's by Sir Frederic Bartlett. Bartlett used a variety of experimental methods, the most famous being the method of repeated reproduction. In this method, subjects were asked to study a story, an argumentative prose passage, or a drawing. After varying intervals of time, they were asked to reproduce the original material. By repeatedly testing his subjects, Bartlett hoped to find "something about the common types of change introduced by normal individuals into remembered material with increasing lapse of time."

Bartlett found that accuracy of report was the exception rather than the rule. His subjects appeared to reconstruct their material, rather than actually to remember it. As a result, the stories of pictures that they would report as "memories" were often quite distorted from the original version. When subjects were asked to recollect material after very long intervals of time (Bartlett calls this "long distance remembering"), the constructive process was particularly evident. All that seemed to remain of the original material were "isolated but striking details."

And even then, the details were remembered only if they fit into the subjects' preconceptions.

Bartlett proposes that we remember by organizing things within the framework of our experiences. Remembering is viewed more as a process of reconstruction than as a recollection. As a result, our organizational scheme relies heavily upon the integration of present experience with that of the past. Sometimes we find it difficult to reconcile the two and, as a result, we often remember what we expected to perceive, rather than that which we actually did perceive.

Bartlett elaborated on these views in his theory of remembering. One of his most important contributions was a discussion of the organization imposed upon stored material: what Bartlett calls a *schema*. His views are quite different from the ones we have been discussing throughout this book. We have continually worried about the nature of the memory trace and the accuracy with which it represents the actual events. Bartlett feels that a memory trace plays a relatively minor role in our recollection of events. We have studied memory of simple items, such as isolated English words. Bartlett studied memory of complex, anecdotal material.

Bartlett found that when his subjects tried to recall stories he had asked them to learn, their versions were shorter, the phraseology more modern, and the entire tale more coherent and consequential than the original. With time these errors increased, but the length of the story that was recalled did not necessarily change. Thus there was much invention, or in Bartlett's terms "constructive remembering." Moreover, his subjects were often unaware that they were inventing rather than remembering, for often the very part that was created anew was the part that the subject was most pleased about and most certain.

These results fit quite beautifully into the structure we have devised to account for the power of mnemonics and organization. It is as if we cannot add anything too new or unique into our memory: things must be introduced gradually, slowly constructed onto the old framework. In many cases, this simplifies our task, for instead of learning all about some new material, we need simply learn how it relates to something already known. The problem with this, as Bartlett showed so dramatically, is that after a while it is not possible to remember what actually did happen—the memory becomes blurred by past experiences.

Bartlett calls a *schema* "an active organization of past reactions, or of past experiences." Various schemata go together into one active, organized setting, all interconnected by common factors. According to

Bartlett, we do not remember by activating some fixed trace of memory image. Rather we reactivate a whole mass of images, we energize the relevant schemata, and we recreate anew the event we are attempting to revive. But in this method, we may err by creating too much, for we may recall what usually was or what ought to have been instead of what really was.

In today's terms we would call Bartlett's schema a rule. Thus we say that much complex behavior is governed by rules, not by rote. For this viewpoint we must thank modern linguistic theory (do we remember the words of a conversation, or do we recreate what must have been said from our memory of the meaning?), but in the present context rules and schemata are one and the same. Bartlett denounces the memory trace, but he cannot escape it entirely, for as soon as we learn something new, no matter how well entwined it becomes with past learned events, something new must be added into memory. We call that something new a memory trace. When Bartlett showed that recollection was primarily reconstruction, he used very complex stories and pictures for his test material. Some of the stories that he had his subjects learn were so involved and unusual that it is not surprising that only the key features were retained. In fact, sometimes even the key features were misperceived. With such difficult material, it is not too surprising that much of what subjects appeared to be recalling from memory was actually made up, reconstructed to fit what little structure had been retained. It is surprising, however, that Bartlett's subjects did not appear to distinguish between material which they did remember and that which they must have reconstructed. How many of our own memories of past events are stored rather than inferred from partial information?

This field needs more research. It would be useful to examine memory for real events; for simple visual scenes; for motor movements; for realistic dramatic events. Many people who play games claim to be able to remember the exact sequence of events that occurred during the game. It would be useful to see how much of this is a true memory and how much a reconstruction. One thing we do know: experts in tasks often appear to have a better memory of what has happened than other people. This apparent superiority of memory can be illusory, however, for the expert not only knows what he should concentrate attention on, but he also knows the basic constraints on the situations. Thus, he can accurately reconstruct complex events from very little information, simply by ruling out implausible happenings. Experts and nonexperts may differ mostly in what aspects they remember, not in how much: one remembers the important things; the other remembers the unimportant.

We are now in a position to summarize some of the characteristics of the memory system. Before we do so, however, it is necessary to hedge a bit on one point. Most of the studies we have examined use verbal material. That is, the material which we have required subjects to learn consists of letters, digits, or words. Thus, our conclusions must apply primarily to situations where the structure of the language is used to assist in the decoding of and memory for events. There is good reason to believe, for example, that the frequent finding of auditory encoding represents more a basic property of linguistic analysis than of memory itself, although the two are obviously very strongly related. Just how much of human performance depends upon linguistic operations is not known, but it is wise at this point to use some caution in extrapolating the present interpretations of human memory.

A number of experimenters have examined memory for form, following the errors and confusions made by subjects in their attempts to reproduce pictures at various times after they had been presented. Although the results of these studies are somewhat inconclusive, they are important for anyone who wishes to continue studying the topics introduced in this chapter. A thorough review of many of these studies is available in the essay by Riley (1962).

The present picture looks something like this. First, for material which enters the visual system, there is a very limited capacity sensory store: *a visual information storage*. Linguistic material in the sensory store is then decoded into an auditory form and maintained in an *auditory information storage* or *primary memory*. The capacity of primary memory is limited by the number of items that are present. Individual items can be maintained in primary memory by frequent rehearsal, that is, by a reactivation of the acoustical properties of the items.

Auditorally presented material appears to go more or less directly to primary memory. There is very little evidence about the properties of a sensory acoustic store analogous to the visual information storage. We do not even know whether or not one exists.

In order for material to be stored within *secondary memory*, it must be integrated within the existing organization: it must fit within the existing schemata. The studies of Bartlett indicate how strongly the organization of material already in secondary memory influences the amount and manner of storage of new material. It is clear that, as a rule, simple images of events do not get stored. The discussion in Chapter 6 on organization and mnemonic systems helps illustrate what must be done in order to make newly acquired information fit within reasonable schemata. We can interpret mnemonic systems as a formal set of techniqués for organizing unrelated material into memory so that later reconstruction is possible.

Brown and McNeill suggest a structure for the memory of words in which we form a dictionary based on the important features. Some physical features of words, particularly length, beginnings, and endings, are attended to more than other features and so are retained better. The selection of features is not arbitrary. Learning the ends of something first is a commonplace psychological phenomenon. Moreover, the English language seems well organized to reinforce this behavior: the longer a word, the better able we are to recognize it on the basis of its length and its ends without knowing anything about the middle.

Brown and McNeill point out that people seem to learn the minimum amount of information needed to enable them to use words. Of course, if we only learn some features of a word poorly, we may be able to recognize the word whenever we need to, but be unable to reconstruct it when that is required. This may be what happened with Bartlett's subjects. They were unable (or unwilling) to memorize his test material *verbatim.* They only encoded what they thought to be the important aspects of the material or what fit easily into already existing schemata. Bartlett's subjects might have been able to perform better had they been given tests for recognition of the material. They were required to recall, however, and as a result, the best they could do was to reconstruct something from the structure they had learned.

8

Models of Memory

In this chapter we investigate models of the memory system which are more precise than the verbal descriptions of the previous chapters. The vehicle of precision is either mathematics or computer programming. Precision is of little use, however, unless the assumptions underlying the models are correct. Unfortunately, as the preceding chapters have illustrated, the description of the processes of sensation, perception, attention, and memory is still in its infancy. As a result, the best that can be done with a formal model is to study how a particular method of approach works for a specific problem. Thus, we must examine many different models, most of which cannot even be compared with one another for they have different purposes and make different assumptions. In this chapter our purpose is to illustrate the possible techniques rather than try to summarize all approaches. We examine only a selected few models in order to cover the variety of techniques which are being used.

BASIC PHILOSOPHY

We start a model by deciding upon the basic operations we wish to study. Then we try to deduce the implications or predictions of these operations. One method of proceeding is to make a verbal prediction, to think through the logical implications and verbally state the form of the expected results. This must always be the first approach used by any investigator, but it is unsatisfactory for a final model, primarily because different people give different interpretations to verbal statements.

A more exact procedure is to translate the theoretical assumptions into mathematical ones, work through the predictions of the mathematics, and then try to translate the mathematical results back into descriptions of behavior. This method of mathematical modeling is precise and free from misinterpretation. Its power is that it makes detailed numerical predictions about many aspects of behavior. A good model can summarize much evidence in a few simple statements. The weakness of this approach, especially in psychology, is that the translation between the observed behavior and the mathematical description is often quite strained. Moreover, many simplifying assumptions must usually be made in order to keep the mathematics in a form that can be solved. The type of simplifying assumptions used are common to many fields other than psychology—assumptions about initial values and the effects of past history, assumptions about symmetry and the interactions of different systems, and assumptions about time-invariance and linearity—and the resulting problems are much the same. (For a discussion of these problems in physics, see Heisenberg, 1967.)

One other way to study the characteristics of a model is to use it to simulate the behavior under study. That is, given the basic theoretical operations, simply follow the result of applying each of them in the appropriate sequence. Thus, the modeler mimics the subject and produces an unambiguous statement of the predicted behavior. In the past these simulations were difficult to do because even a simple model with a limited set of assumptions has hundreds of possible combinations of these assumptions and hundreds of possible stimulus conditions, making tens of thousands of possible predictions. The tracing out of all possible interactions of the model was too tedious to be done completely. With the introduction of modern digital computers and, particularly, with the arrival of sophisticated programming languages, simulation of very complex processes can now be done in a very short time.

Simulation is superior to mathematical analysis in that the number and nature of assumptions necessary to test a model are much reduced. Simulation does offer its own peculiar set of problems, however. For example, consider how we must handle one typical problem by computer simulation and by mathematical modeling. Consider a model which says that under certain conditions the subject determines his response by guessing. In a mathematical model we could represent the subject's guessing probability by the variable g. The solution to the problem would be an equation with an explicit reliance on g, regardless of the particular numerical value it might happen to have in any particular case. Thus, to determine what would happen were the subject suddenly to double the probability of guessing the answer, we look at the final equation and see the result. When simulation is used things are different. Simulations, at least at the present time, must be performed on specific cases. Thus, a simulation must use a particular numerical value for the guessing probability. Then, to see how changes in the guessing probability change behavior, a specific new numerical value must be assumed and the whole process fed back to the computer for a new simulation.

Let us now examine several examples. In this examination, no attempt is made to provide a comprehensive picture of models of memory. Rather, the attempt is to provide representative samples of the direction in which the theorizing is proceeding. The work discussed will all be very recent, for it is in the nature of science that the life span of any theory is short.

A COMPUTER SIMULATION

A convenient start is with a description of a simulation of a fundamental phenomenon of verbal learning and memory experiments: the serial position curve. The first model, "A theory of the serial position effect" by Edward Feigenbaum and Herbert Simon (1962) illustrates several things. For one, it emphasizes the strategies used by subjects and tries to incorporate the effects of these strategies directly into the model. For another, it is an excellent illustration of the techniques of computer simulation in general.

The aim of these authors is to demonstrate the behavior that must result from a few simple assumptions about the way humans process information. They show how a few simple assumptions about information processing leads naturally to a basic experimental fact: the serial position effect. This is a model at a high level of abstraction. Presumably, someday we would produce a more detailed model to describe how the types of information processing postulated here are developed from more basic mechanisms, and then an even more detailed model describing how these mechanisms come about from more elementary structures, and so on, *ad infinitum.*

Before we begin the simulation attempt of Feigenbaum and Simon it would be wise to detour slightly in order to get some background material about the psychological phenomenon under study. The most important background paper is a study of serial position curves by John W. McCrary, Jr. and Walter S. Hunter (1953). In this paper, McCrary and Hunter point out some of the critical properties of the serial position curve that, it turns out, make the simulation process successful.

The experiment under study is one of ordered recall. Basically, the subject is shown a list of words (one at a time) and then must reproduce them in the same order as he initially saw them. This procedure is repeated as many times as are necessary for the subject to learn the entire list. Usually the procedure is modified so that there is no real distinction between presentation trials and recall periods by the use of an anticipation procedure. As the subject sees one word, he is asked to recall the next. Then that word is presented, and the subject must recall the one that will follow, and so on until the subject demonstrates complete accuracy in his predictions. When we look at the number of errors that a subject makes in learning each individual item before he masters the complete list, we see the results form a bow-shaped function, commonly called the serial position effect. That is, most errors are made in the middle of the list and very few are made to words at the two ends. These serial position curves have been studied almost *ad nauseum* in psychology by varying every aspect of the experiment imaginable. McCrary and Hunter point out that all the results seem to have remarkable consistency, if only they are looked at properly. The figures which show the percentage of total errors that occur at each serial position are identical, regardless of which of the many variations of the experiment is being examined. This remarkable similarity of functions led Feigenbaum and Simon to attempt to find the common factor in all the experiments. In doing this, they aimed not only to describe the data, but also to construct a model that fit our intuitions about the underlying processes. In particular, they tried to incorporate features such as the apparent single-mindedness of the attention mechanism and the limited capacity of short-term memory. Thus, although the phenomenon directly under study (the serial position effect) is not really of direct relevance to the topics discussed in this book, the form of model created by Feigenbaum and Simon is.

The nature of the phenomenon being clear, the next step is to specify the approach. Feigenbaum and Simon hypothesize that ". . . serial learning is an active, complex process involving the manipulation and storage of symbols by means of an interacting set of elementary information processes." This particular set of descriptive words is not calculated to invoke much surprise from the reader, but it does set the stage for the approach. As they point out, subjects work hard at the learning process. If we ask a subject what he is doing during all the time he spends at the learning task (or if we introspect at our own behavior in the situation) we find that he tries to establish relations among the various items to be learned: mnemonics, associations, all the processes discussed in earlier chapters. The subject is thwarted, however, by two basic limitations: (1) the limited span of attention makes it difficult to attend to every item that is to be learned, and (2) the limited primary memory span makes it difficult to retain many items.

The model tries to work directly with the stated strategies of subjects in an attempt to piece together the sequence of operations followed in the learning task. A number of postulates are combined with the strategies and the final result, a list of procedures followed and difficulties encountered, is used to direct the simulation of human behavior. The processes suggested by Feigenbaum and Simon are familiar ones; we have encountered all the ideas before in the chapters on attention and primary memory and in the discussion on how things are learned, stored and retrieved. The very important contribution of their model is the way in which these concepts are fitted together to produce a statement about behavior. Unfortunately, even the simulation procedure as carried out on a modern computer has its limitations, so the notions of attention and memory are very much simplified from the complexities discussed earlier in the book.

Now, to the first point. Subjects take a long time to learn material. What are they doing during all that time? Hovland (1938) estimated that it took a subject an average of about 30 seconds to memorize each item on the list. Yet, it only takes a few tenths of a second for humans to respond to words—why this enormous discrepancy between the time to understand and respond to a word (in a conversation, for example), and the time to memorize it? This large amount of time suggests a great deal of complexity in the operations going on during the storage of the material.

The model proposed by Feigenbaum and Simon consists of four postulates. These describe (1) a serial attention mechanism, (2) an average processing time for each item, (3) an immediate memory capable of holding only 5 or 6 symbols, and (4) a statement about the sequence of processing the individual items on the list. Most of these postulates are familiar to us, although they are somewhat simplified to their essential features by Feigenbaum and Simon in order to keep the model at a reasonably simple level of complexity. The one that is somewhat new is postulate 4, the statement about processing strategy. Feigenbaum and Simon suggest that subjects learn from anchor points. That is, starting with some unique item—such as the one at the beginning or end of the list—learning proceeds by picking up items adjacent to these anchor points. This technique reduces the load on immediate memory, because "at each stage of the learning task, the next syllable (item) to be learned is readily identified as being adjacent to a syllable (item) that has already been learned. Thus, no special information about position in list needs to be remembered." This description, then, is of a mechanism building up a memory for the list from the two ends, working slowly toward the middle. This, of course, is exactly the notion of clumping or categorization described in Chapter 6.

As you can guess from this description, the predictions of the model are rather easy to work out; it turns out that the computer is not needed at all. The predictions are remarkably good. This simple con- catenation of statements about the role of attention, memory, time, and learning strategy describes the growth of the serial position curve with remarkable accuracy. Even if this model represents a tremendous simplification of the actual processes, it cannot be denied that the spirit of the operation has been captured.

The description given so far is sufficient to program the computer (or to work out the predictions by hand, without the computer, if you so desire). Before we discuss the results of the simulation, let us digress briefly to consider a topic of great concern to all model builders: free parameters. When the model has been developed in its final, rigid form, often we leave available a few places where we can hedge a bit, adjusting the details of the prediction to fit the observed data as well as the restrictions of the model allow. Each place where this is possible is called a *free parameter*. In classical physics, for example, the laws of acceleration of projectiles have one free parameter, g, the acceleration produced by the earth's gravitational field. We adjust the value of g to fit our observations best. We must vary the value when we move to the moon or another planet. The more free parameters, the more one distrusts the model. The parameters give freedom to make the predictions fit any data, whether or not the model (or the data) makes any sense. These parameters are not all powerful, of course, for the format of the particular model imposes restrictions on the type of pre- dictions that can be made: if the velocity of a falling body does not increase linearly with time, no adjustment of the parameter g will save the model.

In psychology, models with no free parameters are rare; models with but one free parameter are occasionally studied, but they are usually not powerful enough to explain much. When the number of parameters gets around five, the model is viewed with suspicion by the model building community. One of the features claimed by the pro- ponents of computer simulation is that they have very few, if any, free parameters in their system. This is both true and false. The problem is that if you know a value of a parameter beforehand, it can be inserted as a fixed quantity into a model, and then, if it is fixed, how can it be called a *free* parameter? This is what happens in the computer model.

There are three places in Feigenbaum and Simon's model for freedom. Consider postulates 2, 3, and 4. Clearly the amount of time required to process each syllable (postulate 2) is one parameter, for the number of errors made in learning a list depend upon its value. The size of immediate memory (postulate 3) is another. In the model it is chosen to be big enough to hold one pair of items. The probability that any specific item adjacent to an anchor point will be selected for learning next is considered to be 1/N, where N is the number of anchor points involved (postulate 4). This probability could be adjusted, if needed, to fit the data. Feigenbaum and Simon only tried to predict the *proportion* of errors made at any serial position, thus the total number of errors is irrelevant and the processing time parameter can be eliminated. The size of immediate memory was also cleverly chosen, so it did not have to be changed. The probabilities of selecting new items did not need to be altered, so that freedom was not used—hence, prediction without any visible free parameters.

The amazing thing about this model is that it does very well. To describe the peculiar bow-shaped curve one gets in a learning experiment would need a mathematical equation containing around three parameters; the simulation model contains none. In its place, of course, is a good deal of structure and rules. Each rule is, in a sense, a parameter.

The model says that we learn from both ends of a list. The proportion of errors we make on an item is given by the number of trials it takes us to get around to attending to that item, divided by the number of trials it takes to cover the entire list. Is this how you learn things? If not, why does the model do so well? In fact, the model also is able to handle the serial position curves obtained when lists are subdivided, for example, by coloring each half of the list a different color. In this experiment more complex results are obtained, but with the addition of one parameter, the simulation does its job quite well.

There have been a number of models of human processes developed through computer simulation. Most of them are not relevant to the topics discussed in this book. One work that may interest some readers, however, is the program called Elementary Perceiver and Memorizer (EPAM) developed by Feigenbaum (1959 and 1963). EPAM has also been written to describe a number of phenomena observed in the study of verbal learning. Its particular feature is the development of a strategy for representing the items which are to be learned through a discrimination network that uses as little information as it can. In fact, the scheme for storage of words given by Brown and McNeill in Chapter 7, used to describe the partial recall obtained during the tip-of-the-tongue state, was borrowed, in part, from the operations of EPAM. We will not discuss this model here, for it would take us somewhat astray from the main subject of our investigations. The purpose of going this far was to describe the philosophy used in this class of models. Simulation methods promise to be an important technique of the future. At the present time the field is still in its infancy and very little has yet been accomplished.

MATHEMATICAL MODELS OF THE MEMORY TRACE

We now turn to an entirely different philosophy of model building. The next several models will be devoted to a mathematical explication of the decaying nature of a memory trace. In what follows, the mathematics will be mostly eliminated. Those readers with good backgrounds in probability theory will have to go to the original papers to find the precise statements of the theories.

A STRENGTH MODEL

We start with a mathematical "strength" theory of the memory trace. This theory, described formally in a paper published in 1966 by Wayne A. Wickelgren and Donald A. Norman still restricts itself to a general description of logical processes, but at a more detailed level than that used in the "information processing" approach. In the strength theory, the emphasis is on the description of the time course of the memory trace. Little attempt is made to consider how this might affect (or be affected by) the strategies of subjects. The model is purely descriptive at an intermediate level of analysis. "How can we describe what happens," the strength theorist asks, "when an item which has just been presented fades from a clear complete image in memory from which retrieval is simple to a weak image from which retrieval is difficult or impossible?"

The strength theorist attempts to describe the way that the memory trace changes with time. He has to describe three things: the initial acquisition of a memory trace; the process of decay; and the rule the subject uses in determining his response. The theory is quite simple. It assumes that when an item is presented to the subject, some representation of the stimulus becomes active in the subject's memory. At first the representation is clear and complete but, as more items are presented, the representation of earlier items become weaker, less clear, and more ambiguous. The multitudinous variables that make up the memory trace can be summarized by a single measure of their accuracy of completeness: memory trace strength. When the strength of the representative of an item is high, we say that the item is remembered well. When the strength is low, we say that it is remembered poorly or not at all. At the time of test, the subject examines the memory strength of the representative of the test item and decides upon his answer from what remains of the memory trace.

The model is designed primarily to describe the results of a particular type of experiment: a recognition memory experiment with controlled rehearsal. A recognition experiment, as we have already seen, is one in which the subject is first presented with a list of items to be learned and then is presented with test items. His job is to decide whether each test item is an *old* one (whether it occurred in the previous list). In the experiments described by the model, only one test item is presented after each list. By controlled rehearsal, we attempt to insure that all items on the list receive equal amounts of processing by the subject. Unless otherwise instructed, subjects tend to spend more time trying to learn the first few items of a list than later items. To eliminate this, we ask subjects to consider and learn each item as it is presented and then, when each new item arrives, to concentrate fully on it without ever thinking of earlier ones. This instruction is difficult to follow, but with practice it can be mastered. These several restrictions are not critical to the specification of the model which follows. They are useful in the preliminary stages of research because they allow the theorist to concentrate on a limited set of problems. But the model can be (and has been) extended to cover tests of memory other than by recognition, experiments in which many test items were presented after each list, and experiments in which the equal rehearsal instruction is not used.

Basically the model describes what happens to the trace strength of an individual item in memory. To start, we assume that when the item is presented in the list, the strength of its representative in memory goes up: call the amount of the increase α. Now, we must describe how the strengths of memory traces change when other items are presented. We do this by letting the presentation of an item which is different from the one under study decrease the strength of the memory trace to some constant fraction (call it ϕ) of its previous value. Thus, if the value of α were 10, then just after k occurs in the list of items, its strength in memory is 10. If ϕ were 0.8, then after one more item had been presented, the strength of k would drop to 8.0. As more and more items were presented, the strength of the trace for item k would decrease further—from 8.0 to 6.4, then to 5.12, and 4.096, and so on, approaching a limit of zero as the number of other items gets infinitely large. If we were to stop the experiment after 3 items had followed the presentation of k, the strength of its memory trace would be 5.12. We might test the subject's memory by presenting the item k and asking the subject if he remembered it. We assume that he decides upon his answer by first examining the current strength value for k. The trouble is that even though the true value of k's strength is 5.12, the whole memory and decision process is assumed to be noisy, and noise might distort things so that the value actually observed was perhaps only 2.0. The problem really arises because if a different test item had been presented, call it x, one which had not occurred in the list, the noise might make its strength momentarily large, say 3.0. The subject does not have our knowledge that k really did occur previously and x did not; he must make his decision entirely on the basis of his observations. The example we have just given is one where a decision rule can be wrong on one or both cases.

This strength theory combines a number of different theoretical ideas. The fading memory trace is an old notion, one which we have discussed in this book in Chapters 4, 5, and 7. The decision theory is also borrowed, this time from research on the methods for detecting small signals embedded in noise: the theory of signal detection. The first application of the decision theory to tests for the recognition of previously learned words was made by James Egan in 1958. Egan, working in the Psychoacoustic Laboratories at Indiana University, recognized that there is much in common between the task of detecting a weak auditory or visual signal which is embedded in noise and recognizing a faint trace from memory. The description of the dynamic changes that occur in the values of memory trace strengths has been borrowed from the techniques of mathematical models of learning. Some readers will note that although the most direct influence on the theoretical ideas have come from the sources just listed, there are strong similarities between these models and the works of earlier investigators, most particularly Hull and Thurstone. But rather than worry about the exact historical precedence of the ideas, let us plunge ahead into the details of the strength model. The original paper by Wickelgren and Norman is rather technical, however, so what follows is adapted from a simplified description of the model (Norman, 1966b).

Three different psychological processes must be represented in the model. In the first process, acquisition, we must describe how material gets into memory. This whole process—which took all of Chapters 2 and 3 to describe—is summarized in this model by the simple parameter

α. The second process is that of memory itself. We represent the forgetting that occurs in primary memory by the single parameter ϕ: the fraction of the memory trace for each old item that remains after each new item enters primary memory. Thus, we can combine the effects of acquisition and forgetting and say that trace strength in primary memory of an item that was presented i items ago is

$$P(i) = \alpha\phi^i. \tag{1}$$

The third process is that of decision. Here the information from the memory stage is analyzed to determine what action shall be taken. It is here that the biases, strategies, and criteria of the human are combined. The exact form of the decision process must vary with the nature of the task expected of it. For example, recognition and recall require different methods of examining the contents of memory, and thus require different decision rules. The interactions of these three systems are shown in Fig. 1.

In the recognition experiment the subject decides whether a test item is old by examining the strength of its representation in memory. If the strength is rather high he has no problems, he should respond *yes*. If the strength is very low he has no problems, he should respond *no*. But what should he do about intermediate strength values? Does the intermediate value indicate that the item was presented but has decayed or that it is a new item in this experiment but still has some residual strength from a previous presentation? How is he to decide? To complicate matters still more, the whole memory and decision process, being physiological in nature, is probably noisy, so that all the strength values seen by the decision system would fluctuate somewhat about their true value. This would mean that sometimes even items that were never presented will have substantial strength.

The problem is illustrated in Fig. 2. In part A of the figure the true memory values for an old and a new item are illustrated. Were this an accurate picture, subjects could always distinguish one from the other. In part B, we see the effects of noise. The observed values of trace strength vary around their true points. Because of this variability, a single observation made at one instant in time is inaccurate. In part C of the figure, the variability is represented in a different fashion. Here we plot the relative frequency that we expect to observe any particular strength value for an old or a new item, given that the true value is represented by part A. The portions of the distributions that overlap considerably are the portions that cause trouble. Part D of the figure illustrates the decision rule that we assume is used by the subject. A particular criterion value of trace strength is chosen as a response cri-

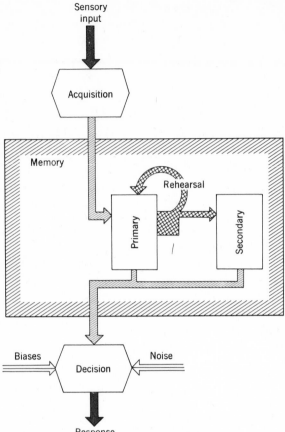

Sensory
input

Fig. 1. Interactions among the three different processes affecting the subject's actions in a memory experiment. In the acquisition process, the sensory input is encoded for the memory process. Items in primary memory are rapidly forgotten, whereas items in secondary memory can be retained for long periods of time. In the decision process, the output of the memory is combined with the subject's biases to determine his response. Noise can be considered to enter the process at this point.

The loop labelled "rehearsal" indicates the effects of this operation: to renew the strengths of material in primary memory and to help enter it in secondary memory.

terion. If the observed strength is greater than (to the right of) the criterion, the response chosen is *yes*, the item is indeed old. If the observed strength is below (to the left of) the criterion, the response chosen is *no*, the test item is not old. The shaded areas of the curves show what percentage of the time correct and false *yes* responses are made. If we know the shapes of the distributions, and if we measure

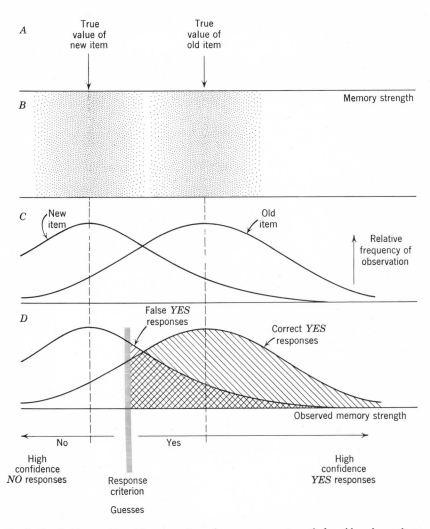

Fig. 2. The decision problem. The true values of memory trace strength for old and new items are shown in A (and by the vertical dotted lines in B, C, and D). The observations of these values continually fluctuate, however, as shown in B, with the observations most frequently being observed around the true values, but occasionally extending far below and above (part C). The decision rule is to establish a response criterion (shown in D) so that every observation above the criterion leads to a "yes" answer. Some of these yes responses are correct, others are false.

the correct and false recognition rate in an experiment, we can determine how far apart the distributions must be from one another. This distance is our estimate for the strength of the memory trace.

Note that the choice of the criterion location is completely up to the subject, but given this location, the probabilities with which he makes correct and false recognitions follow immediately from Fig. 2. Note also that this decision rule guarantees that he will make mistakes, both of omission and of commission. If the subject wishes to decrease the number of errors he makes when responding *yes*, he can do so by moving his criterion to the right, but at the expense of an increase in the number of errors when he says *no*. Similarly, he can decrease the number of times he fails to recognize an old item by moving the criterion to the left, but at the expense of an increase in the number of false *yes* recognition responses. Because the subject can completely alter his behavior simply by shifting the criterion without any change in what he actually has remembered, the number of correct responses is as much a function of his decision processes as it is of his memory process.

Under this decision process the subject can tell us much more about his memory than the simple *yes* or *no* response would indicate. For one thing, he can judge the correctness of his response. Whenever the representation of the test item has a high strength in memory, he can answer *yes* easily and with high confidence. If the representation has a very weak strength he can answer *no* with high confidence. Intermediate strengths have intermediate confidences. Thus, if the subject responds with confidence ratings as well as his *yes-no* response, the memory strength axis of Fig. 2 can be partitioned into a number of different regions, each indicating different confidence ratings and, hence, memory strengths. If the subject is asked to use 5 confidence judgments there are 10 different response-confidence combinations and 9 criteria partitioning the strength axis.

An illustration of the way the probabilities observed in an experiment are transformed into the decaying trace strengths described by Eq. 1 is shown in Fig. 3. These data come from an experiment in recognition memory. The subject was presented with a sequence of 7 different three-digit numbers. At the end of the sequence a test number was presented and the subject was asked to decide whether or not he thought the test number had appeared in the list. Figure 3(a) shows the probability that he correctly answered *yes* for the seven possible values for i. The dotted lines show his false recognition rate: the probability that he said *yes* when the test digit had not been presented in the list. In Fig. 3(b) these response probabilities have been converted into strengths by the method

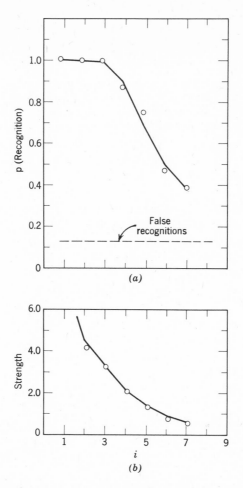

Fig. 3. (a) Probability of a correct recognition as a function of the number of items intervening between presentation and test (*i*). The false recognition probability is shown by the dotted lines. (b) Estimates of memory trace strength for these data. The solid lines show the theoretical predictions of Eq. 1.

described. The solid line through the points is the estimated theoretical decay function of Eq. 1.

In tasks other than recognition, the subject must use different decision strategies. In some recall experiments, for example, the subject is given a cue to the correct item, but nothing else. He must decide from the cue what action to take. Consider the experiment in which the subject is given a list of stimulus items followed by a test item. He is assured that the test item always occurred exactly once in the preceding stimulus list. His job is to respond with the item that followed the test item in the list. This task is different from that of the recognition experiment, because in recognition the strength of the test item can be used directly to determine the response. In recall, however, it is the strength of the associations to the test item that must be used. If all possible responses are well known by the subject, he can examine the strength of the forward association from the test item to each possible response and choose the item with the largest strength of association. Even though the association strengths in recall are probably different from the item strengths in recognition, it seems reasonable that they might follow much the same laws, both in the way that they decay with the presentation of other items and the way in which they fluctuate with added noise. If there are k different responses to the test item then the probability of correct response is given by the probability that the strength observed for the correct item is greater than the strengths observed for each one of the $k-1$ other items.

An inherent part of the decision process is the ability of the subject to decide how accurate his response really is. Outside of the laboratory, people might very well attach different actions to the different regions of response strengths from those forced upon them by the experimental psychologist. For example, rather than give a response in which he had low confidence, a person would probably refuse to take any action at all or, at least, try to get more information before acting. But whatever the differences in behavior observed in and out of the laboratory, the strength model of memory and the criterion model for decisions seem consistent with our intuitions of the memory process and with behavior.

The strength theory tries to summarize the dynamics of memory. It ignores the difficult issues of understanding exactly what and how material is stored, but it does summarize a way that many different processes—acquisition, attention, retention, decision—can interact to determine the probability that an item which is present can later be retrieved. The theory can indeed be extended to include the effects of various testing procedures, but there is no need to discuss the variations here. The important point for our present purposes has been made: namely, a possible characterization of the memory trace.

A MULTICOMPONENT MODEL

A different approach to the theoretical specification of memory is provided in the next model. Its author, Gordon Bower of Stanford University, provides a more detailed analysis of the components of the memory trace. By comparison with the other models we have discussed, Bower attempts to specify the way by which the distributions used in the strength theory come about. Although Bower's work and his results differ somewhat from that of strength theories, the differences are not basic ones, so that one would hope that these theories would eventually become compatible with each other, differing only at the level at which each attempts to specify the memory process. In a sense, Bower provides the rationale for the assumptions used in the strength theory analysis (Bower, 1967).

Bower's model illustrates one of the differences between loose, verbal models and precise, formal ones. In verbal statements of models it is easy to overlook complications that result from the implications of statements that appear clear and unambiguous. Mathematical models allow no such leeway: the ambiguities must be resolved if the model is to work. This formalization can be both bad and good. It is good because we are forced to consider all the implications of the model, some of which are sometimes missed in simple verbal statements. It is bad (a better word might be "embarrassing") because most of the ambiguities turn out to revolve around issues about which we have little or no knowledge. Thus, although we can specify the exact assumptions involved in a mathematical model, some of these are bound to be quite arbitrary, chosen simply in order to keep the model going.

As we examine Bower's model we will come across several such choice points. Bower identifies them for us and, at least in two places that we examine, resolves them by taking several alternative solutions. As a result the one model soon becomes two, and then four, as we take more and more options about our choice of assumptions. These various models are all very similar, so we might conclude that we are studying a *class* of models rather than a single instance of one. This means, of course, that all the models we study in this chapter should really be treated as examples of a style of approach, and the specific assumptions and statements of the models should not be considered to be as important as the general method being proposed.

We shall now examine Bower's work. We examine his model in sufficient detail to give some feeling for the procedures he adopts, but we leave just before the mathematical derivations start.

We start with a picture of memory very much like that shown in Fig. 1. We want to describe how the encoded representation of the stimulus is stored. It is assumed that when a stimulus input goes through the acquisition state, a pattern recognition process extracts a number of attributes or features through stimulus analyzing mechanisms. We can now consider the stimulus as being represented by an order list of attributes, where each attribute might take on any one of a number of values. Bower distinguishes between two levels of encoding. The first, which he calls primary, is the list of attributes that have just been described. The other, which he calls secondary, is the recognized, meaningful form of the primary code. Thus, were we to present an English word visually, the set of visual parameters extracted by the visual stimulus analyzing mechanisms would constitute the primary code. If the word had to be vocalized, either in order to be recognized or simply as part of the general characteristics of the immediate memory system (as described in Chapters 3 and 7), then the list of vocal features would be the secondary code. We have discussed this type of distinction throughout the book, although never in these terms. What is important for an understanding of Bower's model is that we can represent an item in memory by an ordered list of attributes.

We now have an ordered list of attributes or components for each item in memory which specify the details of the particular features used for its encoding. Any list of this kind can be treated mathematically as a vector, with the first element in the list being the first component in the vector and the ith element of the list corresponding to the ith component of the vector. For an experiment in which the subject is asked to learn some item B, the theory is concerned with how B gets encoded into a vector of components and how the individual components of that vector change as forgetting occurs. The description of the forgetting of the components leads to our first choice point: which of the many possible schemes of forgetting should we use?

What is forgetting? It must represent some loss of confusion of information stored in each component vector. But how do we represent this loss? To start with, we need some assumptions. Bower starts by saying that loss of component information proceeds in an all-or-none fashion. That is, either a component is there or it is not—there are no in-between states allowed. Of course, since the component vector contains many individual elements, the loss of information in the overall trace will appear to be graduated in many small steps.

Now, how do we use the degraded information? When we wish to recall an item, Bower assumes that forgotten elements of the component vector are randomly assigned values. What this means, of course, is that there will be errors in recall. But the errors will follow exactly the sort of confusions that are in fact observed. If recall is delayed some components will have been forgotten, but sufficient correct components remain so that the actual output will have many features in common with the correct response. Hence, for words, the errors will be acoustically related to the original; for stories, the meaning may be similar, but the details wrong.

Bower still needs to specify the forgetting process more exactly before he can proceed with the model. There are several ways to proceed. Bower compromises by choosing two different methods. Yet another problem arises: how are lost elements to be treated in the recall process? Again Bower hedges, taking two courses. Thus, we now have four models. Let us examine here the two directions of component forgetting: hierarchical or independent.

By the hierarchical scheme, Bower supposes that the elements of the component vector can be strictly ordered in importance. Then, he assumes that least important elements are the first to be forgotten. To determine the probability of recall, we need to know the probability of losing a component at any instant of time and, then, how many components we can expect to have retained at any time. The basic statement of these probabilities are simple: the actual solutions of the equations that result are difficult.

By the independent loss scheme, Bower supposes that all elements of the component vector are of equal importance and show equal resistance to forgetting. This statement of forgetting leads to a much simpler set of equations than the hierarchical scheme. Whether it is more accurate is hard to tell.

Bower now works out in detail the ways that the components of the vector deteriorate with time, the probability distributions of ending up with specified numbers of components, and the probabilities of retrieving the correct material. He does this for a wide variety of conditions, including both recognition and recall experiments, and experiments with different numbers of response and stimulus alternatives. The theory is very complete in its ability to describe a number of different phenomena. Unfortunately, it does not seem possible to describe it in any more detail than we have already done without immediately getting involved in the mathematical derivations. The main features of the model have been stated: the representation of the memory trace as a multidimensional vector where individual components represent different attributes of the stored image. Deterioration of the memory trace is viewed as the forgetting of the individual elements of the component vector. The decision problem is concerned with trying to reconstruct the possible stimulus item that is represented by the partial memory trace.

The process of model building is something of a game, with the builder attempting to choose assumptions that not only sound reasonable to the psychological public but that also maintain the mathematical structure at a workable level. Many reasonable sounding assumptions lead to equations which either are nonlinear or have time-varying parameters: either case being areas of mathematics that are not well developed.

The main differences between the strength and multicomponent theories lie in the level at which the processes of memory are portrayed. Strength theory arbitrarily assumes the existence of memory traces and distributions. The multicomponent model does not make these assumptions, but, in its place, it must assume an even larger and more complex set of assumptions about the individual components of the theory. At some future date, when we have learned more about the processes underlying memory, we will be able to decompose Bower's assumptions about components of the memory trace into still more basic (but probably a larger number of) statements. It is clear that eventually we need theories which describe the whole process of memory. Today, with our limited experimental and theoretical knowledge, it is difficult to defend one level of theorizing as more basic or elegant than another: they all require a number of assumptions about the nature of underlying mechanisms.

We have now examined in brief outline two different models of the memory trace. These limited samples do not by any means exhaust the possibilities: many different examples could have been selected. The two that were chosen, Wickelgren and Norman's strength model and Bower's multicomponent model, do illustrate most of the basic principles used by the modelers. Although when viewed from close up there is a wide range of techniques being used; from a distance the models do not really differ by much. That is to say, the general frameworks, assumptions, and problems are similar; the particular assumptions made and the type of mathematical structure assumed do differ.

One other model ought to be mentioned, however, for it does differ somewhat from what we have already seen. This is the structural model proposed by R. C. Atkinson and R. M. Shiffrin (in press). In their model, Atkinson and Shiffrin attempt a grand synthesis of many of the ideas discussed in the earlier chapters of this book. They clearly separate structural features of the memory system—the processes assumed to operate in a diagram such as Fig. 2—from control processes—the flexible plans and strategies discussed in Chapter 6. Then, they develop models of the structural aspects which can differ in operation, depending upon the particular control scheme in use. Of particular interest in their models is the concept of a new type of storage system: a rehearsal buffer. Their model explicitly incorporates the results of various rehearsal strategies, with the strategies coming from the control system and the results depending upon the workings of the structural system.

The final version of their model—not yet represented in their published descriptions—will probably involve a combination of computer simulation and mathematical methods. Computer simulation seems best suited to handle descriptions of strategies and control processes; mathematical modeling seems best for describing the workings of structural processes.

PROBLEMS IN RETRIEVAL

The models we have looked at so far are concerned primarily with the acquisition, storage and retention of information. It is clear, however, that the process of retrieving information, both from short- and long-term memory, plays an important role in the memory process. Retrieval, especially from long-term memory, has been almost completely ignored by formal models of memory, and for good reason. Until we are able to specify the mechanics of the earlier stages it makes little sense to attempt grand theories of memory. Even with this caution, however, it is tempting to speculate on possible descriptions of retrieval from a large-capacity storage system.

Anyone who has searched unsuccessfully in a library for the reference to a book realizes that the major problem with large memories is organization and retrieval rather than storage. In most storage systems, whether they be libraries, computer memories, or human memories, each item that is stored can be described by several different properties: its contents, its address or actual location in the storage, and its associations or relations with other stored material. Only one property—the address—can actually be used to get to the material. Other information is useful only in helping get to the address.

Storage in a library has been organized to make discovery of relevant material relatively easy. First, the address scheme tells something about the stored material: books on similar topics are stored in locations near each other. But even so, the physical organization of the library seldom can be used as a retrieval technique. The next important item in the library is the card catalog, a small library in its own right. The catalog, like all indexes, is simply a miniature version of the library, containing less information than the contents of the books, but adding information about their locations. Searches of card catalogs are successful only if enough information is known about the sought-for-item to make it possible to find it in the catalog cards. Many index systems are available in libraries, but they all have the same basic properties: they are condensed, reorganizations of the library.

One of the most important properties of human memory is that it has a very efficient retrieval scheme. Normally our search for a word or name is so fast that we are not aware of the mechanics which are involved. True, sometimes we stumble, with the sought-for-information at the "tip of our tongue" but not quite retrievable. Other times we remind ourselves of something we had previously stored (saying "oh yes, now I remember"), indicating that any earlier failures to remember the material were failures of retrieval. The usual event, however, is that we immediately determine whether events were learned previously or not, indicating that we can go rapidly to the proper addresses of stored information. Whatever actual operations are involved, it is quite clear that they must include the logical equivalents of our library search, except for much more efficient cross-indexing and access to stored material.

We frequently are able to recognize immediately when we are confronted with a novel situation. If shown a new word—this chapter emphasizes the mantiness of memory—we know that the word is new. This ability to scan rapidly through memory and reject novel items has some strong implications about the method of reaching the stored addresses of material which is in memory. The point is simple: "mantiness" does not exist in your memory, hence your ability to discover this fact indicates that you did one of two things. Either you scanned the entire contents of memory and discovered the absence of "mantiness" or you examined that part of memory where the word "mantiness" would have been, had it been present, and discovered its absence. The first hypothesis can be rejected as implausible. Human memory is just too large to allow such a search, even if we could examine all our memories simultaneously (we return to this issue later). The second alternative also seems implausible, but at least conceivable. It means, however, that we are able to use either the sound or the sight of the word "mantiness" to get to the part of memory where it ought to be stored. Thus, we can say that the address of a word can be determined entirely by its physical characteristics. Note the peculiar implication: even things which we have never experienced before already have a specific memory location reserved for them. This is not to be taken as a statement concerning prior knowledge; it is only a description of the sensory orientation of memory.[1]

[1] Do not misinterpret this argument as implying that specific information **may be** stored in specific physical locations within the brain. This may be true, **but it**

The rapid rejection of novel words can be contrasted with the very slow recognition of real words. The best example of the latter is the tip of the tongue phenomenon, which we have already examined. Although there appears to be no formal evidence on this point, it must follow that even in the tip of the tongue (and related) phenomena we can tell rapidly whether or not we have ever known the item for which we seek. Although it may take a long time to recover all the information about an item from memory, the immediate rejection of novel words must be accompanied by an immediate acceptance of old ones. This whole argument, by the way, does not require that all novel words be rejected immediately. As long as we are able to do so properly with a few, the rest of the argument must follow. Note, if you will, that by now you should have rather rapid recognition of "mantiness": try yourself on "mansuetude." The latter, my dictionary informs me, really is a word.)

COMPUTER SEARCH TECHNIQUES

When access to the contents of memory can be based on the structure of the sought-for-material, we say that the memory is addressable by content. The examples we have just discussed, combined with other, related considerations, argue that human memory is a content-addressable storage. In the computer field, content-addressable stores are highly desirable, but, as yet, uneconomical. They are difficult devices to construct, for the natural way of storing and retrieving material in a memory is to use the physical features of the memory (get the item which is in location number 26240) rather than the contents (get the meaning of the word "mansuetude") or features of the material. There are several ways by which content-addressable storage can be implemented. One is to let the form of the material be the address. For example, suppose we wish to store the dictionary definition of a word. The word must first be encoded into some standard form. Consider for a moment how this is done by a digital computer. The sequence of letters is represented internally by a sequence of binary digits. This string of binary digits can

may also be false: we do not know. When we discuss the logical properties of human memory, it is convenient to talk about the storage of specific items and the logical addresses and locations of these items. But these words stand for the procedure for getting back the information stored in the memory, whether that information be at a specific physical location or scattered about. The actual physical (including, of course, physiological, neurological, and chemical) implementation of memory is quite irrelevant to the present discussion, indeed, to much of the book.

be interpreted either as a number or as letters—which we do depends upon the set of instructions that the computer is told to follow. (One of the most important properties of computers is that they make no distinction in their memory between instructions, numbers, and letters. Thus any operation possible by the computer can be performed on anything that is stored.) Now, if we interpret the sequence of binary digits used to encode the word as a number rather than as letters, we can use that number as the address of the word we seek. If information about a word is stored physically in the address specified by the form of the word, retrieval is easy. When one searches for the meaning of a word, one thinks of the word, interprets that word as an address, and then retrieves the material located at that address. Then, if the information that has been retrieved is not completely satisfactory, we can use some of the items that have been retrieved to form the address for our next search of memory; this process can be repeated as often as necessary to get the desired material.

There is one obvious major difficulty with a memory scheme organized by the representation of its stored information: the memory has to be large enough to have a unique address for every possible input. This requirement can be relaxed by using only a part of the input to specify the address or by transforming the item into a code which has a reduced number of possible combinations. Schemes of this sort (sometimes called "hash coding") must provide ways of avoiding problems when different items produce the same address.

A good deal of analysis might precede the search of human memory before a sensory representation of an item determines its address in memory. It is clear that the physiological outputs of the various sense organs go through a set of stimulus analyzing mechanisms which extract a variety of specific features of the sensory event. Whether special combinations of features excite unique locations or unique configurations in the memory system is not known, but it is clear that a feature analysis would improve performance. In any event the initial access to the memory must be based entirely on sensory analysis. Nothing else can be used, for nothing else is known about the sensory input until it has been analyzed.

A second way of developing a content-addressable store is to search all the contents of memory. This can be done, in principle, by any device simply by systematically searching memory, stopping when the location which is being examined matches the input. Searches of this form are unrealistic; the average amount of time required for the search increases linearly with the size of the memory. If the search could be done by a parallel device—that is, all memory locations scanned at the same time—

the problems of organization of memory would be much reduced, for no longer would material have to be stored systematically. Whether some content-addressable storage is used in human memory is questionable. The issue is simple: its properties are suggestive of the properties of human memory, but there is no evidence one way or the other.

One other problem of storage concerns the way in which related material is linked together. These links or associations among stored material play a very important role in the memory process because they allow us to get to all the material related to the original item, rather than just the limited information stored with the item itself. The links are necessary because related material gets stored at different times; without some kind of formal link, the relationship between material dealing with apparently different topics and stored at widely separated intervals would only be recovered with great difficulty. Links can be represented in a memory by several techniques, the most popular computer technique being to store "pointers" along with the information. These pointers contain addresses of related material, so that when any stored item is retrieved it will be accompanied by addresses of related items. There are many schemes devised for using these pointers. Often, the pointer refers either to the item directly preceding or following the stored item, so that the pointers link together a file. These files (or lists) form the basis of several simulations of human cognitive processes (see Newell and Simon, 1963; Feigenbaum and Feldman, 1963; Reitman, 1965).

A number of techniques for storing and retrieving large amounts of data are now being studied by workers in the computer sciences. At the present time, however, their results have little to offer us: the human memory still exceeds any machine memory both in overall capacity and in speed and flexibility of retrieval. The techniques now under study, moreover, do not differ in any substantial way from those just discussed. Data are represented in files or in tree structures. Relations among stored data are represented by pointers that link files, either by the simple linkages described here or by more complex threaded list procedures. Sometimes the relations are simply stored in indexes: a separate index for each possible way of using memory. These inverted indexes (as they are called) are somewhat related to the dual-indexing scheme of a thesaurus.

AN ANALOG MODEL OF WORD ASSOCIATIONS

A different, though related procedure is described in the next selection by Vincent Giuliano. The purpose of Giuliano's paper is to describe a device for maintaining associations among references to documents. His goal is to devise a system which would let a researcher choose a few key words which are descriptive of a problem and then, by entering the system with these key words, find documents relevant to the research. The concept of key words did not originate with Giuliano. It is a standard technique used by almost every system of document retrieval. Our special interest in Giuliano's specification of the problem comes from the nature of his particular model for searching the stored references: his techniques are suggestive of processes of human memory.

Giuliano emphasizes a statistical approach to word association problems and describes a mathematical description and an electronic model which he has built and tested. We skip the mathematics here (the interested reader can examine the original article) but present the electronic model in sufficient detail to give some feeling for the way it operates.

ANALOG NETWORKS FOR WORD ASSOCIATION *

VINCENT E. GIULIANO

Before proceeding with the technical discussion, two areas of possible applications of word association techniques will be mentioned.

The first example is from the area of automatic document information retrieval. Suppose that, within the context of an automated information center, large numbers of documents are indexed according to key words they contain, and that these index terms are then recorded on magnetic tape for subsequent searching by a computer. In particular, suppose that document **A** has to do with the *Oxidation* of *Ferrous Materials* in *Saline Solutions,* and is indexed with the three italicized key terms. At some later point, a requestor

* Vincent E. Giuliano. Analog networks for word association. *IEEE Transactions on Military Electronics,* 1963, **MIL-7,** 221–225. With permission of author and publisher.

may come to the center and ask for all documents on the *Rusting* of *Iron* in *Sea Water*. If the computer finds nothing on searching, who is to blame for the failure to locate document A? Obviously, it is not the requestor's fault, for he has accurately stated his own interests. Likewise it can hardly be considered to be the indexer's fault, for he could not be expected to anticipate every possible way that his document could be requested. The facts of life are that natural language allows many alternative ways of expressing the same semantic content, and that there is in general no one unique way of expressing a given thought. Clearly what is needed is a means of automatically recognizing associations present among words, so that requests with roughly equivalent meanings will retrieve roughly the same documents.

The second example is somewhat more speculative, and is drawn from the area of machine translation. Suppose that a computer is programmed to translate from English to, say, Russian, and it comes upon the English word "bank,"—should this word be translated as "Банк" (financial institution) or as "Берег" (shore or water bank)? The answer to this question cannot be found by investigating formal lexical or syntactic clues; it must depend on the semantic content of the neighboring context. Obviously, if "bank" is found in conjunction with such words as money, finance, loans, mortgage, checking, etc., the first interpretation is preferable, but if it is found with words like boat, water, river, etc., the second is to be preferred. The example suggests that knowledge of association patterns of words might be highly useful in resolving semantic ambiguity in machine translation—the major stumbling block in the current state of this art.

The need for methods of semantic association brought out in both of these examples follows from the fact that the meanings of words are richly overlapping. It is difficult (if not impossible) to find two words which are synonymous under all interpretations. This is well known by writers who struggle to avoid repetitious use of a single word. What is more surprising is that it is difficult to find two words with completely disjoint meaning. The reader may be interested in doing the following experiment: pick two words A and B at random, and find the "distance" between them in "Roget's Thesaurus" as follows: find all the classes that A belongs in and all those that B belongs in. If A and B both fall in a common class, then consider the distance between them to be zero. If not, look up all the words in the classes A belongs to and all the words in the classes B belongs to; if one of the A words falls in a common class with one of the B words, then consider A and B to be separated by distance one. Likewise, if a word of distance one from A falls in the same class with a word of distance one from B then consider A and B to be separated by distance two, etc. What then is the reader's guess as to the average minimum distance between two randomly selected words? Distance ten? One hundred? It is probably more like two or three. At least this has been so in the few tries made by the author. The game is a bit arduous, but the reader is invited to try it for himself. It is surprising how quickly one can go in this manner from a given word to one of opposite meaning! For example, "extortion" is distance one from "valor" via the chain: *extortion*—parsimony (819)—*tenacity*—courage (861)—*valor*. In fact, all substantive words in natural language are more or less associated; the real question is how much more or less, and that is the subject of this paper.

SYNONYMY AND CONTIGUITY ASSOCIATION

This paper is basically concerned with word association based upon formal statistical properties of a limited body of language data, the goal being to define an objective procedure for determining numerical measures of association strength among words present within a given set of contexts. Before proceeding, however, it is necessary first to say a few words on what might be meant by the association measures.

To start with, it seems reasonable that a useful measure of association should model synonymy, i.e., similarity of meaning among such terms as "canine" and "dog," "lamp" and "light," "elephant" and "pachyderm," etc. But is synonymy association all that is required? Obviously, if this were the case, associations could be established by compiling a thesaurus (treasure of words), and listing within the thesaurus estimated strengths of synonymy between related word pairs. Indeed, major efforts have been made recently on the compilation of thesauruses for such applications as automatic information retrieval.

Unfortunately, though, the thesaurus approach to word association is beset with certain fundamental difficulties which stem from the nature of language itself. The first difficulty is that there is rarely such a thing as complete synonymy. Synonymy, when it is found, is almost always partial and extremely difficult to measure. A wolf is a canine but not a dog; some lamps are not lights and some lights are not lamps, etc. A second difficulty is even more fundamental: synonymy is not the only kind of association present among words. In fact, for many applications it may not even be the most important kind of association. This is because synonymous expressions are readily constructible of nonsynonymous components or parts, which are nonetheless associated. It is simply not possible to anticipate beforehand all such possible combinations of words which yield synonymous expressions. As an example consider the two expressions, "Coherent Optical Radar," and "Pulsed Laser Reconnaissance Device," the two expressions are nearly synonymous under a certain interpretation, but none of the individual words in the first expression can be considered to be synonymous with any of the individual words in the second expression without a stretch of imagination, i.e., the expressions are synonymous, but the parts are not!

The example of the last paragraph suggests that a second type of word association should be considered, association which is primarily due to close real-world relationships among the objects or actions which the words designate. Examples of this type of association are those between "table" and "top," "hammer" and "nail," "food" and "eat," "bank" and "money," etc. This type of association has been called contiguity association by psychologists, since the objects or properties denoted by the words are presumed to be contiguous in some sense in the real world. Now, considering the example from the last paragraph from the contiguity viewpoint, "coherent" and "optical" both bear contiguity relationships with "pulsed" and "laser," and "radar" bears contiguity relationship with "pulsed," "reconnaissance" and "device." The situation is illustrated in Fig. 4, where the expressions "Coherent Optical Radar" and "Pulsed Laser Reconnaissance Device" are shown to have multiple paths of contiguity cross association. Under one interpretation, the expressions "Coherent Optical Radar," and "Pulsed Laser Reconnaissance Device" have the same meaning, although no words in the first expression are synonyms of any in the second. By considering the combined effect of multiple contiguity association paths between the words, however, the two combinations may be recognized as being highly associated with one another.

This example raises a question: Is there a possibility of combining a number of possibly weak contiguity associations among words, so as to strongly associate combinations of words which have closely related meanings, but which do not associate in the word-by-word synonymy sense? Obviously, it is not possible to accomplish this end by anticipating every possible combination of contiguities in a thesaurus compiled beforehand. Fortunately, however, an entirely different approach to the recognition of associations exists, and statistical methods such as those described below can give measures of association which reflect the effects of contiguity as well as synonymy.

— — —

Some workers on computer-based word association schemes apply their formulas twice or more—once to expand to "first generation" words once re-

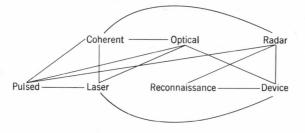

Fig. 4. Example of combination of contiguity association paths.

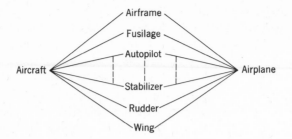

Fig. 5. Example of two synonymous words which are unlikely to co-occur but which are likely to have similar co-occurrence patterns with other words.

moved from a given word, once to expand the "first generation" words to obtain words twice removed from the given word, etc. The reason for doing this can readily be seen in the example illustrated in Fig. 5. In the example, it is presumed that many contexts contain "aircraft" together with words from the center list, and that many other contexts contain the word "airplane" together with words from the center list, but that no context contains both "aircraft" and "airplane." Such might well be the case, for example, if the contexts are documents and the words are used as index terms to characterize documents; some indexers may use "airplane," others may use "aircraft," but few will use both to characterize the same document. A human who knows no English (say a clever Chinese) could infer from studying the co-occurrence patterns of these words within their context that "aircraft" and "airplane" are highly associated. He might even go on to speculate that they are somewhat synonymous since they appear to be used interchangeably in similar contexts.

— — —

LINEAR ASSOCIATION AND LINEAR ASSOCIATIVE NETWORKS

The Method

This section is devoted to a brief discussion of a "linear" method of automatic word association under development by the writer and his colleagues. The method offers a number of novel features; among these are: (1) it offers a systematic framework for recognizing indirect as well as direct statistical associations among words, (2) the method offers a framework for modeling mathematically not only associations but also relevance, a difficult-to-grasp concept which is at the heart of such fields as document information retrieval, and (3) the technique lends itself to realization by means of an analog network memory, and association can be performed in parallel by means of such a network without a need for sequential digital scanning. Moreover, such a network need involve only passive resistive or capacitive elements and can therefore in principle be constructed at a small fraction of the cost of a conventional digital memory.

Mathematical equations of the linear association process can be arrived at through any one of at least three parallel avenues of reasoning: (1) reasoning based upon the imposition of certain mathematical constraints on the association transformation, primarily consisting of certain assumptions of the linearity and normalizability of transformation matrices, (2) reasoning along probabilistic lines, in which association is regarded to be a certain type of Markov process, and (3) reasoning based upon an intuitive development of an electrical network analog. All three approaches are ultimately equivalent in that they lead to the same set of mathematical relationships for the association process. The approaches differ in the interpretation they provide; each gives a different avenue of appeal to intuition. The electrical network approach will be pursued in the next few pages, since it can be presented using nonmathematical arguments.

— — —

Development of the Linear Association Technique

The Case Without a priori *Word Connections:* Suppose that, at a given time, a fixed number of contexts and words are recognized within the scope of a particular application, and that each context is essentially indexed by only those words which best characterize it. Suppose further that it is possible to assign a positive numerical connection strength between a context and each of the words which applies to it. Although these values can all be equal in the simplest case, they need not necessarily be so restricted. This situation is illustrated graphically in Fig. 6, where diamonds represent contexts, circles rep-

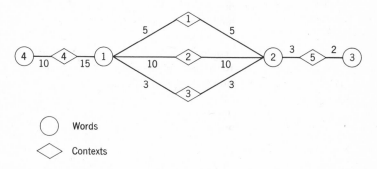

Fig. 6. Graph showing connection strengths between a few contexts and words.

resent words, and the numbers next to the links represent relative connection strengths between the contexts and the words. Thus, the context-word configuration can be conceptually represented by a network. There may be only one direct path between a context and a word, but there may be a multiplicity of indirect paths. To obtain the electrical circuit analog, each context node and each word node in the context-word graph is considered to represent an electrical binding post, and each connection is considered to be a resistor with conductance equal to the connection strength. Finally a set of "leak" resistors (say with conductance values presumed to be small compared to any of the word-context conductances) would be affixed between each node and some common return "ground" node.

— — —

So far, nothing has been said about how such a network can be actually used to associate. To adopt a general viewpoint, an association transformation can be considered to consist of an input, consisting of a given assignment of positive or negative values to one or more selected words which are of interest, and a resultant output consisting of values assigned to *all* words and contexts recognized within the association system. For the association process to be meaningful, the output value assigned to a word should reflect its relevance to the given configuration of input words and values. The more relevant it is, the higher should be its value.

In the electrical analog, the input consists of fixed currents injected into the terminals for the given input words, with return being the ground terminal. The input values are merely the values of the currents injected; they need not necessarily be all equal, and may in fact be of opposite signs when anti-association is desired. The output values are simply the voltages appearing on the various terminals in the network, both for words and for contexts, as a result of the currents being applied to the input word terminals. Corresponding to the values appearing on the terminals, they will be effectively ranked according to the decreasing order of these values. This ranking is taken to define the relative association, *i.e.*, the relevance of any given item to the input configuration is determined by the voltage appearing on its terminal.

The behavior of the network can be grasped at this point. When currents are injected into some of the terminals, namely the terminals for those words specified on input, voltages appear on all of the terminals in the network, both those for words and those for contexts. The voltage appearing on any word terminal will depend on how strongly that word is connected with the words in the inquiry via all direct and indirect paths. The further a word is in the network from a word in the input, the lesser will be the voltage appearing on its terminal. Three parallel paths exist between words 1 and 2 in the circuit of Fig. 7, for example, and therefore a current injected into the terminal for word

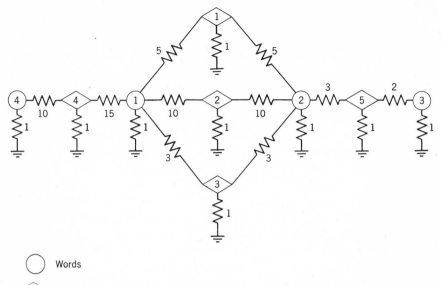

Fig. 7. Electrical network obtained from graph in Fig. 6. (Numbers next to resistors represent conductances.)

1 will induce a high voltage on the terminal for word 2, and a relatively low voltage on the terminal for word 3. Words are thus automatically associated depending on their degree of direct and indirect connections with each other.

The over-all association coefficient between a given pair of words is thus seen to be the voltage response at the terminal for one word to a unit of current injected at the other word, or, in terminology more familiar to electrical engineers, the transfer impedance between the two terminals. As is known by a reciprocity theorem of electrical networks, transfer impedance is a symmetric function so that the association between words A and B is the same as that between B and A.

Of course, injection of currents into terminals for selected words in an input also results in all of the terminals for contexts assuming greater or lesser positive voltages. The voltage appearing on the terminal for a context will depend on: (1) how strongly that context is connected to words specified in the input, and (2) how strongly that context is connected to other words which are in turn strongly connected to words in the input. The voltages on the context terminals will therefore give a ranking of the contexts according to their association with the input words. Such a voltage can also be considered to model the relevance of a context to an input.

In the case of document information retrieval, when the contexts are documents and the words are used as index terms, the input represents a combination of terms which state the interests of a literature searcher. The linear association process ranks all documents according to a continuous scale of relevance with respect to the search question, utilizing in the determination of relevance not only words present in the actual question, but also words highly associated with these. Presumably, the documents of greatest interest to the searcher will be among those listed topmost in this ranking.

Giuliano has proposed a scheme for using an electrical network to determine the associations among words and context. Although his ideas are designed primarily for an automatic information retrieval system, the structure he proposes is very appealing to those psychologists who like to consider human memory as an interconnected network of information links. The details of the implementation are not important; the links among items could be made by the storage of relevant addresses as well as by actual physical connections suggested by Giuliano, however, the determination of relevance by a consideration of the *total* interconnections between any two items is important.

Statistical associations have limitations. The structure of language, for example, is governed by the application of rules, not by the relative frequency with which we use words. The statistical structure mirrors the results of the application of linguistic rules in our language behavior. Associations probably play an important role in our ability to use language—both in speaking and in listening—but we should not fall into the trap of thinking that they are sufficient to handle all the situations that we encounter. Even so, a good deal of our memory is highly interconnected; Giuliano suggests a possible model for describing the links.

This chapter has reviewed, at a very basic level, a wide variety of models concerned with a variety of phenomena. We have barely scratched the surface, however, for there are many more mathematical models under study than we have examined. One large class of these models is related to the strength and multicomponent models of Bower, Norman, and Wickelgren. Most of them, however, are more directly related to the recent studies of mathematical models for learning. The emphasis in most (though not all) is on the probability that an item will be transferred between various internal states of learning, the states being named by terms such as *learned, short-term memory,* and *guessing.* The discussions in this chapter exhaust neither the existing models nor the ones possible in the future. Although the four models which have been discussed do illustrate the procedures used in the majority of studies, the choice of the particular ones examined has been somewhat arbitrary. The creation of good models to describe the processes of memory and attention offers some of the most exciting possibilities in the future of psychology.

SUGGESTED READINGS

There are many directions one can follow in continuing the work discussed in this Chapter. Three different classes of models have been discussed: (1) computer simulation, (2) probabilistic models, and (3) information retrieval.

A summary of work on computer simulation is contained in the collection of reprints edited by Feigenbaum and Feldman (1963). The books by Hunt, Marin, and Stone (1966) and Reitman (1965) describe particular implementations of models, neither, however, directly related to memory or attention. See also the comments on the philosophy of EPAM by Feigenbaum and Simon (1963). An extension of EPAM is given by Hintzman (1968).

Mathematical models come in many varieties. To examine models of memory, in addition to the papers by Atkinson and Shiffrin (in press), Bower (1967), and Wickelgren and Norman (1966) discussed in this chapter, one can look at recent papers by Bernbach (1965, 1967), Bower (in press), Kintsch (1966, 1967), Norman (1966a), and Norman and Wickelgren (1965). There are others, but these provide a start. For an introduction and discussion of the decision models used in the trace models, see Green and Swets (1906).

A convenient source of advanced models of memory (both computer simulation and mathematical models) is the book edited by Norman (in press).

Information systems have been studied a good deal in the computer literature under the terms "data management system" and "information retrieval system." Some papers relevant to these areas are to be found in the book by Meadow (1967) and the collection of papers edited by Schecter (1967). Also see the papers of Douglas (1966), Landauer (1963), Prywes (1966), and Prywes and Gray (1963). In addition, the paper by Prywes (1961), in conjunction with Prywes and Gray (1963), should be of interest. Here Prywes compares human capabilities with those of computer systems. In this context, also see Miller (1956b). A good introduction to the problems of maintaining linked lists can be found in Chapter 2 of Knuth (1968).

The journals where most work relevant to models of memory can be found are:

The Journal of Mathematical Psychology
Psychological Review
IEEE Transactions on Electronic Computers
Communications of the ACM

and the various spring and fall computer meetings, such as, *Proceedings of the Spring Joint Computer Conference* (*SJCC*).

Finally, *Computing Reviews* publishes critical short reviews and abstracts of all papers, books, and theses relevant to the information sciences, including many papers in the field of psychology.

9

In Retrospect

In the preceding chapters we have examined the ways in which verbal information gets processed by humans, starting with the mechanism of selective attention and concluding with a discussion of the problems involved in storage and retrieval. In all these discussions there has been a common theme, making it possible to incorporate these various operations into one comprehensive picture of human information processing. In this final chapter, let us review briefly much of what has been discussed, this time combining and generalizing the theoretical picture until we arrive at a comprehensive story.

All paths lead to memory. The organization of the book was designed to follow the flow of information from the environment through the human. Thus, we started by discussing attention and pattern recognition, hoping then to introduce various types of memory systems in a systematic, gradual order: visual information storage, primary memory, secondary memory. This natural progression of events was not possible. Each system seemed to depend upon the properties of all the others. In fact, it would have been possible to have organized this book differently. We could easily have started with a discussion of the general principles which underlie large capacity, permanent memory systems. Then, by asking two questions—How does material get stored?, How does material get retrieved?—we could have arrived at all the issues discussed in this book.

We started our discussion in Chapter 2 with attention: our ability to extract the one message of concern out of many that might simultaneously be present. This selective ability is also a limitation, for we are unable to do more than a very limited number of complex activities at the same time. We choose the message to which we attend by selectively restricting our attention to those physical cues and meaningful contents that we think will be relevant. We can lose the message if either the physical or the meaningful cues change or are interfered with by other, distracting messages.

How are we able to use the meaning of messages as cues to their selection? Two possible mechanisms emerged from the discussions. One suggested that physical signals were selected for further attention solely on the basis of their physical characteristics. However, as the meaning of a message was determined, the system that examined the physical features became biased toward certain broad classes of inputs which might be expected to arrive. In this way, meaningful signals might sometimes receive full attention even though they would normally have been rejected from consideration. The other possible mechanism of attention allowed all signals to be analyzed for their meaning (although crudely), with selection for further processing occurring afterwards. This system requires that the sensory features of incoming signals be sufficient to allow them to reach their representation in memory.

Both proposals have in common heavy reliance on feedback of information from the analysis of current events to predictions about future events. One puts the burden of complexity upon the physical extraction of information from the physical features, the other puts most of the difficulties on an automatic access to memory by sensory events. Either system requires an enormous amount of interaction with memory; predictions about the future cannot be made without an understanding of the present, and that understanding must come about through an interpretation of events based upon information stored in the past.

In Chapter 3 we looked at the extraction of information from the incoming signals. Most of these studies fall under the title of "pattern recognition" and we emphasized the problem of speech recognition. Pattern recognition cannot easily be separated from a consideration of selective attention, for if our selection is based upon the meaning of signals, the act of recognizing may not be distinguishable from the act of selection.

In our analysis of pattern recognition, some types of evidence seemed to require that the analysis of incoming sensory events was performed automatically and efficiently: a passive analysis. Recent evidence about the nature of physiological analyzing mechanisms indicates that they are capable of extracting a surprising amount of basic general properties from sensory signals. Other types of evidence, however, seem to require that the analysis be performed by continually attempting to internally synthesize properties to match those of the signals being analyzed: an active analysis. This active process seems necessary to describe the ease with which we deal with ambiguous, incorrect, or missing information, often not even noticing imperfections. No passive model can do this.

Evidence for both passive and active systems leads us to suggest that both may actually be present. We can suppose that passive devices, in particular, stimulus-analyzing mechanisms, are able to extract sufficient information about sensory signals to restrict the set of possibilities to a small, manageable number. Simultaneously, we suppose that an active device can use the meaning, context, and expectations extracted from previously analyzed material to reduce the number of possible signals that need be considered at any time to a small, workable set. If we combine the set of possible items proposed by the stimulus analyzing mechanisms with the set proposed by the active analyzing procedure, we should find the overlap of items to be very small, perhaps unique. Thus, by combining features of active and passive models we may have the best of both worlds; even their occasional failures appear to be consistent with our intuitions.

By allowing the analysis of the unattended, nonselected signals to proceed passively and automatically, we are able to see how important information can sometimes attract our attention, even if we are not consciously processing that source of signal. Because passive systems seem capable only of performing a rough analysis of information, our reactions to signals to which we are not attending should show the following errors: sometimes we should fail to respond to relevant material; sometimes we should respond falsely to material which has no relevance; and always we should fail to extract meaning from material which requires the integration of several different words.

This picture of pattern recognition fits beautifully into the structure postulated for memory. Events to which we are not attending can get access to memory through the structure which allows retrieval through sensory cues. But these events will be neither properly nor fully understood, for understanding requires more than simple extraction of the individual parts. Normally these events will not be remembered, for the requirements of the retrieval process dictate that unless information can be properly organized, later retrieval will fail. Events to which we do not consciously attend cannot receive the proper analysis and organization which is necessary for both complete understanding and retrieval.

Our questions about memory led us to suspect that the organization of stored material is a crucial aspect of its operations. This organization, moreover, has several implications of its own. For one, it must be possible to identify spoken and written words rapidly, primarily through an analysis of their physical characteristics. Thus, we have suggested that the memory system must be organized, in part, around these features of stored material. For another, efficient retrieval of stored material requires an involved storage procedure. The proper integration of new material within the old requires the formation of indexes and connecting links in the storage system. If we are to do this organization before material can be efficiently entered into memory, then we require temporary storage buffers to hold incoming sensory material until it can be properly interpreted, for even an efficient retrieval system takes time to operate—sometimes more time than the actual duration of the sensory event.

We discussed some properties of these storage buffers in Chapters 3 and 4. Chapter 3 introduced the topic and concentrated on a sensory system: visual information storage. In Chapter 4 we considered some of the properties of a different temporary storage system: primary memory. Primary memory appears to be a small, limited-capacity system. Storage appears to be based on meaningful units or "chunks."

The limited capacity of primary memory may play a decisive role in determining the organization of our large capacity secondary memory. If primary memory serves as a working storage, maintaining newly arrived information until it can be successfully integrated within the structure of secondary storage, then the limitations of the former pass on to the latter. This would mean that material in permanent memory is categorized or otherwise grouped into clusters of no more than five to seven items, for that is all that can pass through the bottleneck of primary memory at any one time.

We must also keep in mind the possibility that the two memory systems may represent different properties of the same physical structure. If we assume that the initial activation of storage causes temporary traces to appear, then this temporary activity may be what we call primary memory. Permanent changes in storage occur only when there has been prior activation of the tempory traces and, probably, cognitive action as well: for example, selection, attention and rehearsal. Thus, the two systems might be very closely related, differing primarily in their temporal properties. Of course, because primary traces are continually changing, whereas secondary traces are passive and permanent, the two storage modes might appear to have quite different retrieval properties.

In Chapters 6, 7, and the latter part of 8, we considered some of the rules that might underlie the efficient use of secondary memory. The principles of organization appear to have been recognized for many centuries in the mnemonic tricks found in the popular literature on memory systems. The requirement that new material be efficiently integrated with old can sometimes cause trouble. Thus, because unfamiliar material is not readily assimilated into memory, we are apt to retrieve what ought to have happened rather than what actually did. When we view a complex event, we may attempt to evaluate it according to previously acquired rules and memories. Thus, we store abstractions and schemata rather than images. Much of what we recollect may actually be a recreation.

Finally, in Chapter 8, we attempted a very general examination of some of the procedures used in modeling the phenomena of the earlier chapters. The treatment was very general, but the methods which we discussed are of critical importance. Without formal, precise statements of the broad conclusions we have stated, the picture we have drawn is still empty of content. It is all very nice to say that proper organization is the key to retrieval, but organization is simply a word. It sounds all right to say that stimulus analyzing mechanisms extract basic features from sensory events and that these features determine how the analysis in memory is performed. Similarly, it sounds proper when we suggest that some active process determines the set of expected events from the context and meaning of presently occurring events. But these statements are suspiciously vague.

Can a system of this sort really work? What features are extracted? How are expectations determined? How is the information from these two sources combined? These questions need to be answered with specific statements, not with the broad generalities of the present book. But, with some exceptions, broad generalities are all that we have. The verbal picture is not necessarily a bad way to start. But unless we are able to pin down more exactly the details of all these processes through a mathematical description or computer simulation, the start will be for naught. Meanwhile, by continuing the search, by combining the efforts of workers in a wide variety of fields—Psychology, Linguistics, Acoustics, Electrical Engineering, Computer and Communication Sciences, and the Neurological Sciences—maybe this book will become obsolete. I hope so.

References

The boldface numbers in brackets at the end of each citation refer to the chapter in which that reference is discussed.

Adams, J. A. *Human memory.* New York: McGraw-Hill, 1967. [5]

Ad herennium, see *Rhetorica ad herennium.* [6]

Arbib, M. A. *Brains, machines, and mathematics.* New York: McGraw-Hill, 1964. (Paperback edition, 1965.) [3, 5]

Atkinson, R. C., & Shiffrin, R. M. Human memory: a proposed system and its control processes. In K. W. Spence, & J. T. Spence (Eds.). *The Psychology of learning and motivation: advances in research and theory.* Vol. II. New York: Academic Press, in press. [8]

Averbach, E., & Coriell, A. S. Short-term memory in vision. *Bell Syst. tech. J.,* 1961, **40,** 309–328. [4]

Averbach, E., & Sperling, G. Short-term storage of information in vision. In C. Cherry (Ed.), *Information theory: Proceedings of the fourth London symposium.* London: Butterworth, 1961 [4]

Baddeley, A. D. The influence of acoustic and semantic similarity on long-term memory for word sequences. *Quart. J. exp. Psychol.,* 1966, **18,** 302–309. [7]

Bartlett, F. C. *Remembering.* Cambridge (England): Cambridge Univ. Press, 1932 [7]

Bernbach, H. A. A forgetting model for paired-associate learning. *J. Math. Psychol.,* 1965, **2,** 128–144. [8]

Bernbach, H. A. Decision processes in memory. *Psychol. Rev.,* 1967, **74,** 462–480. [8]

Bousfield, W. A. The occurrence of clustering in the recall of randomly arranged associates *J. gen. Psychol.,* 1953, **49,** 229–240. [6]

Bousfield, W. A., & Cohen, B. H. The occurrence of clustering in the recall of randomly arranged words of different frequencies-of-usage. *J. gen. Psychol.,* 1955, **52,** 83–95. [5, 6]

Bousfield, W. A., & Sedgewick, C. H. An analysis of sequences of restricted associative responses. *J. gen. Psychol.,* 1944, **30,** 149–165. [6]

Bower, G. H. A multicomponent theory of the memory trace. In K. W. Spence, & J. T. Spence (Eds.), *The psychology of learning and motivation.* Vol. I. New York: Academic Press, 1967. [8]

Bower, G. H. Notes on a descriptive theory of memory. In D. P. Kimble (Ed.), *The proceedings of the second conference on learning, remembering, and forgetting.* New York: New York Academy of Sciences, in press. [8]

Broadbent, D. E. Speaking and listening simultaneously. *J. exp. Psychol.*, 1952, 43, 267–273. [2]

Broadbent, D. E. *Perception and communication.* London: Pergamon Press, 1958. [2]

Brown, J. Some tests of the decay theory of immediate memory. *Quart. J. exp. Psychol.*, 1958, 10, 12–21. [5]

Brown, J. Information, redundancy, and decay of the memory trace. In *The mechanization of thought processes.* London: H. M. Stationery Office, 1959. [5]

Brown, R., & McNeill, D. The "tip of the tongue" phenomenon. *J. Verb. Learn. Verb. Behav.*, 1966, 5, 325–337. [7]

Carmichael, L., Hogan, H. P., & Walter, A. A. An experimental study of the effect of language on the reproduction of visually perceived form. *J. exp. Psychol.*, 1932, 15, 73–86. [5]

Cherry, E. C. Some experiments on the recognition of speech, with one and with two ears. *J. acoust. Soc. Amer.*, 1953, 25, 975–979. [2]

Cherry, E. C., & Taylor, W. K. Some further experiments on the recognition of speech with one and two ears. *J. acoust. Soc. Amer.*, 1954, 26, 554–559. [2]

Cicero, M. T. *De oratore.* With an English translation by E. W. Sutton, completed, with an introduction, by H. Rackham. Cambridge: Harvard Univ. Press, 1942. [6]

Cicero, M. T. *De inventione.* With an English translation by H. M. Hubbell. Cambridge: Harvard Univ. Press, 1949. [6]

Cofer, C. N. *Verbal learning and verbal behavior.* New York: McGraw-Hill, 1961. [5]

Cofer, C. N. On some factors in the organizational characteristics of free recall. *Amer. Psychologist*, 1965, 20, 261–272. [6]

Cofer, C. N., & Musgrave, B. S. (Eds.). *Verbal behavior and learning: Problems and processes.* New York: McGraw-Hill, 1963. [5]

Cohen, B. H. Recall of categorized word lists. *J. exp. Psychol.*, 1963, 66, 227–234. [6]

Conrad, R. Errors of immediate memory. *Brit. J. Psychol.*, 1959, 50, 349–359. [7]

Conrad, R. An association between memory errors and errors due to acoustic masking of speech. *Nature*, 1962, 196, 1314–1315. [7]

Conrad, R. Acoustic confusions and memory span for words. *Nature*, 1963, 197, 1029–1030 [4]

Conrad, R. Acoustic confusions in immediate memory. *Brit. J. Psychol.*, 1964, 55, 75–83. [7]

Conrad, R. Order error in immediate recall of sequences. *J. Verb. Learn. Verb. Behav.*, 1965, 4, 161–169. [7]

Conrad, R., & Hull, A. J. Information, acoustic confusion and memory span. *Brit. J. Psychol.*, 1964, 55, 429–432. [7]

Deutsch, J. A., & Deutsch, D. Attention: some theoretical considerations. *Psychol. Rev.*, 1963, 70, 80–90. [2]

Deutsch, J. A., Deutsch, D., Lindsay, P. H., & Treisman, A. M. Comments on "selective attention: perception or response?" and reply. *Quart. J. exp. Psychol.*, 1967, 19, 362–367. [2]

Deutsch, S. *Models of the nervous system.* New York: Wiley, 1967. [5]

Douglas, C. W. File organization and search techniques. In *Annual Review of Information Science and Technology.* New York: Interscience Publishers, 1966. [8]

Egan, J. P. Recognition memory and the operating characteristic. Indiana Univ. hearing and communication lab. AFCRC-TN-58-51, AD-152650, 1958. [8]

Erdmann, B., & Dodge, R. *Psychologische Unterschungen Uber Das Lesen auf Experimenteller Grundlage.* Halle: Niemeyer, 1898. [4]

Fant, G. Auditory patterns of speech. In W. Wathen-Dunn (Ed.), *Models for the perception of speech and visual form.* Cambridge: MIT Press, 1967. [3]

Feigenbaum, E. A. An information processing theory of verbal learning. Santa Monica: The Rand Corp. Paper P-1817, 1959. See also Feigenbaum, 1963. [8]

Feigenbaum, E. A. The simulation of verbal learning behavior. In E. A. Feigenbaum, & J. Feldman (Eds.), *Computers and thought.* New York: McGraw-Hill, 1963. [8]

Feigenbaum, E. A., & Feldman, J. C. *Computers and thought.* New York: McGraw-Hill, 1963. [8]

Feigenbaum, E. A., & Simon, H. A. A theory of the serial position effect. *Brit. J. Psychol.,* 1962, **53**, 307–320. [8]

Feigenbaum, E. A., & Simon, H. A. Brief notes on the EPAM theory of verbal learning. In C. N. Cofer, & B. S. Musgrave (Eds.), *Verbal behavior and learning: Problems and processes.* New York: McGraw-Hill, 1963. [8]

Giuliano, V. E. Analog networks for word association. *IEEE Transactions on Military Electronics,* 1963, **MIL-7**, 221–234. [8]

Green, D. M., & Swets, J. A. *Signal detection theory and psychophysics.* New York: Wiley, 1966. [8]

Grey, J. A., & Wedderburn, A. A. I. Grouping strategies with simultaneous stimuli. *Quart. J. exp. Psychol.,* 1960, **12**, 180–184. [2]

Halle, M., & Stevens, K. Speech recognition: a model and a program for research. *IRE Transactions on Information Theory,* 1962, **IT-8**, 155–159. [3]

Hebb, D. O. Distinctive features of learning in the higher animal. In J. F. Delafresnaye (Ed.), *Brain mechanisms and learning.* London: Oxford Univ. Press, 1961. [5]

Heisenberg, W. Nonlinear problems in physics. *Physics Today,* 1967, **20**, No. 5 (May), 27–33. [8]

Hellyer, S. Supplementary report: frequency of stimulus presentation and short-term decrement in recall. *J. exp. Psychol.,* 1962, **64**, 650. [5]

Hintzman, D. L. Explorations with a discrimination net model for paired-associate learning. *J. math. Psychol.,* 1968, **5**, 123–162. [8]

Hovland, C. I. Experimental studies in rote learning theory. III. Distribution of practice with varying speeds of syllable presentation. *J. exp. Psychol.,* 1938, **23**, 172–190. [8]

Hubel, D. H., & Wiesel, T. N. Receptive fields of single neurones in the cat's striate cortex. *J. Physiol.,* 1959, **148**, 574–591. [3]

Hubel, D. H., & Wiesel, T. N. Receptive fields, binocular interaction, and functional architecture in the cat's visual cortex. *J. Physiol.,* 1962, **160**, 106–154. [3]

Hunt, E. B., Marin, J., & Stone, P. J. *Experiments in induction.* New York: Academic Press, 1966. [8]

James, W. *The principles of psychology.* New York: Henry Holt and Co. 1890. (Also reprinted by Dover Publications, Inc., 1950.) [2, 4, 5, 6, 7]

Kahneman, D. Method and theory in studies of visual masking. *Psychol. Bull.,* 1968, in press.

Katona, G. *Organization and memorizing.* New York: Columbia Univ. Press, 1940. [6]

Katz, J. J., & Fodor, J. A. The structure of a semantic theory. *Language,* 1963, 39, 170–210. [7]

Keppel, G., & Underwood, B. J. Proactive inhibition in short-term retention of single items. *J. Verb. Learn. Verb. Behav.,* 1962, 1, 153–161. [5]

Kintsch, W. Recognition learning as a function of the length of the retention interval and changes in the retention interval. *J. math. Psychol.,* 1966, 3, 412–433. [8]

Kintsch, W. Memory and decision aspects of recognition learning. *Psychol. Rev.,* 1967, 74, 496–504. [8]

Knuth, D. E. *The art of computer programming.* Reading: Addison-Wesley, 1968.

Kolers, P. A. Three stages of reading. In H. Levin, & J. Williams (Eds.), *Basic studies of reading.* New York: Harper, in press. [3]

Landauer, T. K. Rate of implicit speech. *Percept. mot. Skills,* 1962, 15, 646. [4]

Landauer, W. I. The balanced tree and its utilization in information retrieval. *IEEE Transactions on Electronic Computers,* 1963, EC-12, 863–871. [8]

Lettvin, J. Y., Maturana, H. R., McCulloch, W. S., & Pitts, W. H. What the frog's eye tells the frog's brain. *Proc. Inst. Radio Eng.,* 1959, 47, 1940–1951. [3]

Liberman, A. M., Cooper, F. S., Harris, K. S., MacNeilage, P. F., & Studdert-Kennedy, M. Some observations on a model for speech perception. In W. Wathen-Dunn (Ed.), *Models for the perception of speech and visual form.* Cambridge: MIT Press, 1967. [3]

Lindgren, N. Machine recognition of human language. *IEEE Spectrum:*
Part I. Automatic speech recognition, March 1965, 114–136.
Part II. Theoretical models of speech perception and language, April 1965, 45–59.
Part III. Cursive script recognition, May 1965, 104–116. [3]

Loess, H. Proactive inhibition in short-term memory. *J. Verb. Learn. Verb. Behav.,* 1964, 3, 362–368. [5]

Loisette, A. *Assimilative memory or how to attend and never forget.* New York: Funk and Wagnalls, 1896. [6]

Mandler, G. Organization and memory. In K. W. Spence, & J. T. Spence (Eds.), *Psychology of learning and motivation.* Vol. 1. New York: Academic Press, 1967a. [6]

Mandler, G. Verbal learning. In *New directions in psychology III.* New York: Holt, 1967b. [6]

McCrary, J. W., & Hunter, W S. Serial position curves in verbal learning. *Science,* 1953, 117, 131–134. [8]

McGeoch, J. A., & Irion, A. L. *The psychology of human learning*. New York: Longmans, Green, 1952. [6]

Meadow, C. T. *The analysis of information systems*. New York: Wiley, 1967. [8]

Melton, A. W. Implications of short-term memory for a general theory of memory. *J. Verb. Learn. Verb. Behav.*, 1963, **2**, 1–21. [5]

Melton, A. W. (Ed.), *Categories of human learning*. New York: Academic Press, 1964. [5]

Miller, G. A. The magical number seven, plus or minus two: some limits on our capacity for processing information. *Psychol. Rev.*, 1956a, **63**, 81–97. [4, 5, 6]

Miller, G. A. Human memory and the storage of information. *IRE Transactions on Information Theory*, 1956b, **IT-2**, 129–137. [8]

Miller, G. A. Decision units in the perception of speech. *IRE Transactions on Information Theory*, 1962, **IT-8**, 81–83. [3]

Miller, G. A., Galanter, E., & Pribram, K. *Plans and the structure of behavior*. New York: Holt, Rinehart and Winston, 1960. [6]

Miller, G. A., Heise, G. A., & Lichten, W. The intelligibility of speech as a function of the context of the test materials. *J. exp. Psychol.*, 1951, **41**, 329–335. [3]

Minsky, M. L. *Computation: Finite and infinite machines*. Englewood Cliffs: Prentice-Hall, 1967. [3]

Mitchell, J. M. Mnemonics. In *Encyclopaedia Britannica*. Chicago: Encyclopaedia Britannica Inc., 1910, **Vol. 15**, pp. 626–628. [6]

Moray, N. Attention in dichotic listening: affective cues and the influence of instructions. *Quart. J. exp. Psychol.*, 1959, **11**, 56–60. [2]

Morton, J. The interaction of information in word recognition. *Psychol. Rev.*, 1969, **76**, in press. [2]

Mowbray, G. H. Choice reaction times for skilled responses. *Quart. J. exp. Psychol.*, 1960, **12**, 193–202. [3]

Neisser, U. *Cognitive psychology*. New York: Appleton-Century-Crofts, 1967. [2, 3, 4, 5]

Newell, A., & Simon, H. A. CPS, a program that simulates human thought. In E. A. Feigenbaum, & J. Feldman (Eds.), *Computers and thought*. New York: McGraw-Hill, 1963. [8]

Nilsson, N. J. *Learning machines*. New York: McGraw-Hill, 1965. [3]

Norman, D. A. Acquisition and retention in short-term memory. *J. exp. Psychol.*, 1966a, **72**, 369–381. [5, 8]

Norman, D. A. Memory and decisions. Proceedings of symposium on Memory and Attention, XVIII International Congress of Psychology, Moscow, 1966b. To be reprinted in *Acta Psychologica*. [8]

Norman, D. A. Toward a theory of memory and attention. *Psychol. Rev.*, 1968, **75**, in press. [2, 5]

Norman, D. A. Memory while shadowing. *Quart. J. exp. Psychol.*, 1969, in press. [2]

Norman, D. A. (Ed.), *Models of memory*. New York: Academic Press, in press. [8]

Norman, D. A., & Waugh, N. C. Stimulus and response interference in recognition memory. *J. exp. Psychol.*, 1968, in press. [5]

Norman, D. A., & Wickelgren, W. A. Short-term recognition memory for single digits and pairs of digits. *J. exp. Psychol.*, 1965, **70**, 479–489. [8]

Peterson, L. R. Immediate memory: data and theory. In C. N. Cofer, & B. Musgrave (Eds.), *Verbal behavior and learning: Problems and processes.* New York: McGraw-Hill, 1963. [5]

Peterson, L. R., & Peterson, M. J. Short-term retention of individual verbal items. *J. exp. Psychol.*, 1959, **58**, 193–198. [5]

Prywes, N. S. Data processing aspects of some psychological experiments. *Percept. mot. Skills*, 1961, **12**, 155–160. [8]

Prywes, N. S. Man-computer problem solving with multilist. *Proceedings of IEEE*, 1966, **54**, 1788–1801. [8]

Prywes, N. S., & Gray, H. J. The organization of a multilist type associative memory. *IEEE Transactions on Communications and Electronics*, 1963, 488–492. [8]

Quintilianus, M. F. *The institutio oratoria.* With an English translation by H. E. Butler. New York: Putnam, 1921. [6]

Raisbeck, G. *Information theory.* Cambridge: MIT Press, 1963. [5]

Reitman, W. R. *Cognition and thought: An information-processing approach.* New York: Wiley, 1965. [8]

Rhetorica ad herennium. (Author unknown.) With an English translation by H. Caplan. Cambridge: Harvard Univ. Press, 1954. [6]

Riley, D. A. Memory for form. In L. Postman (Ed.), *Psychology in the Making: Histories of selected research problems.* New York: Knopf, 1962. [7]

Sanders, A. F. (Ed.), *Attention and performance.* Amsterdam: North-Holland Publishing Co., 1967. (A special edition of *Acta Psychologica*, Vol. 27.) [2]

Schecter, G. (Ed.), *Information retrieval: A critical view.* Washington: Thompson Book Co., 1967. [8]

Slamecka, N. J. *Human learning and memory: Selected readings.* New York: Oxford Univ. Press, 1967. [5]

Sperling, G. A. The information available in brief visual presentation. *Psychol. Monogr.*, 1960, **74**, Whole No. 498. [4, 5]

Sperling, G. A. A model for visual memory tasks. *Hum. Factors*, 1963, **5**, 19–31. [4, 5]

Sperling, G. A. Successive approximations to a model for short-term memory. In A. F. Sanders (Ed.), *Attention and performance.* Amsterdam: North-Holland Publishing Co., 1967. (A special edition of *Acta Psychologica*, Vol. 27.) [4]

Sutherland, N. S. Stimulus analyzing mechanisms. In *Symposium on the mechanization of thought processes.* London: H. M. Stationery Office, 1959. [3]

Titchener, E. B. *Lectures on the elementary psychology of feeling and attention.* New York: Macmillan, 1908. [2]

Treisman, A. M. Verbal cues, language and meaning in selective attention. *Amer. J. Psychol.*, 1964, **77**, 206–219. [2]

Treisman, A. M., & Geffin, G. Selective attention: perception or response? *Quart. J. exp. Psychol.*, 1967, **19**, 1–17. (Also see Deutsch, *et al.*, 1967.) [2]

Tulving, E. Subjective organization in free recall of "unrelated" words. *Psychol. Rev.*, 1962, **69**, 344–354. [6]

Tulving, E. Intratrial and intertrial retention: notes towards a theory of free recall verbal learning. *Psychol. Rev.*, 1964, **71**, 219–237. [6]

Tulving, E., & Pearlstone, Z. Availability versus accessibility of information in memory for words. *J. Verb. Learn. Verb. Behav.,* 1966, **5**, 381–391. [6]

Uhr, L. (Ed.), *Pattern recognition.* New York: Wiley, 1966. [3]

Wathen-Dunn, W. (Ed.) *Models for the perception of speech and visual form.* Cambridge: MIT Press, 1967. [3]

Waugh, N. C. Free versus serial recall. *J. exp. Psychol.,* 1961, **62**, 496–502. [5]

Waugh, N. C., & Norman, D. A. Primary memory. *Psychol. Rev.,* 1965, **72**, 89–104. [5]

Waugh, N. C., & Norman, D. A. The measure of interference in primary memory. *J. Verb. Learn. Verb. Behav.,* 1968, in press. [5]

Weinland, J. W. *How to improve your memory.* New York: Barnes and Noble, 1957. [6]

Wickelgren, W. A. Distinctive features and errors in short-term memory for English vowels. *J. acoust. Soc. Amer.,* 1965a, **38**, 583–588. [7]

Wickelgren, W. A. Acoustic similarity and intrusion errors in short-term memory. *J. exp. Psychol.,* 1965b, **70**, 102–108. [7]

Wickelgren, W. A. Distinctive features and errors in short-term memory for English consonants. *J. acoust. Soc. Amer.,* 1966a, **39**, 388–398. [7]

Wickelgren, W. A. Phonemic similarity and interference in short-term memory for single letters. *J. exp. Psychol.,* 1966b, **71**, 396–404. [7]

Wickelgren, W. A. Associative intrusions in short-term recall. *J. exp. Psychol.,* 1966c, **72**, 853–858. [7]

Wickelgren, W. A., & Norman, D. A. Strength models and serial position in short-term recognition memory. *J. math. Psychol.,* 1966, **3**, 316–347. [8]

Woodrow, H. The effect of type of training upon transference. *J. educ. Psychol.,* 1927, **18**, 159–172. [6]

Woodworth, R. J., & Schlosberg, H. *Experimental psychology.* New York: Holt, 1958. [6]

Yates, F. A. *The art of memory.* Chicago: University of Chicago Press, 1966. [1, 6]

Young, M. N. *Bibliography of memory.* Philadelphia: Chilton Co., 1961. [6]

Index